W9-DDQ-069

# The Rights of Animals

# The Rights of Animals

Other books in the Current Controversies series:

The Abortion Controversy
Alcoholism
Assisted Suicide
Biodiversity
Capital Punishment
Censorship
Child Abuse
Civil Liberties
Computers and Society
Conserving the Environment
Crime
Developing Nations
The Disabled
Drug Abuse
Drug Legalization
Drug Trafficking
Espionage and Intelligence Gathering
Ethics
Family Violence
Free Speech
Garbage and Waste
Gay Rights
Genetic Engineering
Guns and Violence
Hate Crimes
Homosexuality
Illegal Drugs
Illegal Immigration
The Information Age
Interventionism
Issues in Adoption
Marriage and Divorce
Medical Ethics
Mental Health
The Middle East
Minorities
Nationalism and Ethnic Conflict
Native American Rights
Police Brutality
Politicians and Ethics
Pollution
Prisons
Racism
Sexual Harassment
Sexually Transmitted Diseases
Smoking
Suicide
Teen Addiction
Teen Pregnancy and Parenting
Teens and Alcohol
The Terrorist Attack on America
Urban Terrorism
Violence Against Women
Violence in the Media
Women in the Military
Youth Violence

# The Rights of Animals

**Auriana Ojeda**, *Book Editor*

**Daniel Leone**, *President*
**Bonnie Szumski**, *Publisher*
**Scott Barbour**, *Managing Editor*
**Helen Cothran**, *Senior Editor*

San Diego • Detroit • New York • San Francisco • Cleveland
New Haven, Conn. • Waterville, Maine • London • Munich

© 2004 by Greenhaven Press. Greenhaven Press is an imprint of The Gale Group, Inc., a division of Thomson Learning, Inc.

Greenhaven® and Thomson Learning™ are trademarks used herein under license.

*For more information, contact*
Greenhaven Press
27500 Drake Rd.
Farmington Hills, MI 48331-3535
Or you can visit our Internet site at http://www.gale.com

**ALL RIGHTS RESERVED.**
No part of this work covered by the copyright hereon may be reproduced or used in any form or by any means—graphic, electronic, or mechanical, including photocopying, recording, taping, Web distribution or information storage retrieval systems—without the written permission of the publisher.

Every effort has been made to trace the owners of copyrighted material.

Cover credit: © Richard T. Nowitz/CORBIS

**LIBRARY OF CONGRESS CATALOGING-IN-PUBLICATION DATA**

The rights of animals / Auriana Ojeda, book editor.
p. cm. — (Current controversies)
Includes bibliographical references and index.
ISBN 0-7377-1818-8 (pbk. : alk. paper) — ISBN 0-7377-1817-X (lib. : alk. paper)
1. Animal rights. 2. Animal experimentation—Moral and ethical aspects.
3. Food animals. 4. Wildlife-related recreation—Moral and ethical aspects.
5. Animal welfare. I. Ojeda, Auriana, 1977– . II. Series.
HV4711.R54 2004
179'.3—dc21 2003048330

Printed in the United States of America

# Contents

## Chapter 3: Should Animals Be Bred for Human Consumption?



## Chapter 4: Should Animals Be Used for Human Recreation?

# Foreword

By definition, controversies are "discussions of questions in which opposing opinions clash" (Webster's Twentieth Century Dictionary Unabridged). Few would deny that controversies are a pervasive part of the human condition and exist on virtually every level of human enterprise. Controversies transpire between individuals and among groups, within nations and between nations. Controversies supply the grist necessary for progress by providing challenges and challengers to the status quo. They also create atmospheres where strife and warfare can flourish. A world without controversies would be a peaceful world; but it also would be, by and large, static and prosaic.

## The Series' Purpose

The purpose of the Current Controversies series is to explore many of the social, political, and economic controversies dominating the national and international scenes today. Titles selected for inclusion in the series are highly focused and specific. For example, from the larger category of criminal justice, Current Controversies deals with specific topics such as police brutality, gun control, white collar crime, and others. The debates in Current Controversies also are presented in a useful, timeless fashion. Articles and book excerpts included in each title are selected if they contribute valuable, long-range ideas to the overall debate. And wherever possible, current information is enhanced with historical documents and other relevant materials. Thus, while individual titles are current in focus, every effort is made to ensure that they will not become quickly outdated. Books in the Current Controversies series will remain important resources for librarians, teachers, and students for many years.

In addition to keeping the titles focused and specific, great care is taken in the editorial format of each book in the series. Book introductions and chapter prefaces are offered to provide background material for readers. Chapters are organized around several key questions that are answered with diverse opinions representing all points on the political spectrum. Materials in each chapter include opinions in which authors clearly disagree as well as alternative opinions in which authors may agree on a broader issue but disagree on the possible solutions. In this way, the content of each volume in Current Controversies mirrors the mosaic of opinions encountered in society. Readers will quickly realize that there are many viable answers to these complex issues. By questioning each author's conclusions, students and casual readers can begin to develop the critical thinking skills so important to evaluating opinionated material.

Current Controversies is also ideal for controlled research. Each anthology in the series is composed of primary sources taken from a wide gamut of informational categories including periodicals, newspapers, books, United States and foreign government documents, and the publications of private and public organizations. Readers will find factual support for reports, debates, and research papers covering all areas of important issues. In addition, an annotated table of contents, an index, a book and periodical bibliography, and a list of organizations to contact are included in each book to expedite further research.

Perhaps more than ever before in history, people are confronted with diverse and contradictory information. During the Persian Gulf War, for example, the public was not only treated to minute-to-minute coverage of the war, it was also inundated with critiques of the coverage and countless analyses of the factors motivating U.S. involvement. Being able to sort through the plethora of opinions accompanying today's major issues, and to draw one's own conclusions, can be a complicated and frustrating struggle. It is the editors' hope that Current Controversies will help readers with this struggle.

---

Greenhaven Press anthologies primarily consist of previously published material taken from a variety of sources, including periodicals, books, scholarly journals, newspapers, government documents, and position papers from private and public organizations. These original sources are often edited for length and to ensure their accessibility for a young adult audience. The anthology editors also change the original titles of these works in order to clearly present the main thesis of each viewpoint and to explicitly indicate the opinion presented in the viewpoint. These alterations are made in consideration of both the reading and comprehension levels of a young adult audience. Every effort is made to ensure that Greenhaven Press accurately reflects the original intent of the authors included in this anthology.

---

*"Animal rights activists lie at the radical end of a wide spectrum of animal advocacy."*

# Introduction

The controversy over whether animals have rights has changed dramatically since philosophers first introduced the idea of animal welfare in the eighteenth century. Centuries ago, radical thinkers proposed that since animals could feel pain and pleasure, people should not cause them to suffer unnecessarily. Over the years, the concept of animal welfare developed into a worldwide movement that involves as many different philosophies as adherents. Beliefs range from the original concept of animal welfare to the relatively new idea that animals have the right not to be used for human purposes.

Until the eighteenth century, animals were primarily viewed as property whose singular purpose was to supply humans with food, labor, and clothing. In the 1870s Jeremy Bentham, an English philosopher and jurist, was the first person to assess whether animals had rights. He claimed that animals were sentient beings—they could feel pain and pleasure—and therefore humans should avoid inflicting unnecessary pain on them. According to Bentham, "The question is not, can they reason? Nor, can they talk? But rather, can they suffer?" Bentham's writings on the rights of animals launched an influential movement that spread throughout the world.

Bentham's philosophy was particularly radical in eighteenth century England, when only humans were viewed as possessing rights. Most people's beliefs were based on traditional biblical philosophy, which taught that God had granted humans dominion over animals. Moreover, burgeoning Enlightenment philosophy held that humans were the only creatures who could reason and therefore were the only possessors of rights. During this time, however, philosophers such as Bentham began to propose that animals had interests of their own, namely to seek pleasure and avoid pain. According to these philosophers, humans had the right to use animals for labor, clothing, and food, but they were also responsible for ensuring that animals did not suffer unnecessary pain in the process. Thus, Bentham and others did not accord animals the same rights as humans but argued that animals at least had the right to be treated humanely. Bentham and other philosophers condemned common leisure activities such as bullbaiting, cockfighting, and dog and cat fighting because they were cruel and inflicted unnecessary pain on animals.

Bentham's philosophical writings gave rise to organizations and legislation created to protect animals. The first animal protection organization was founded in England in 1824 and became known as the Royal Society for the Prevention of Cruelty to Animals (RSPCA). Its goals were to ensure humane treatment of animals, reduce animal cruelty, support the enforcement of existing animal welfare legislation, and help get passed new laws that protected animals' wellbeing. In addition, the British Parliament passed an act in 1835 to "consolidate and amend the several laws relating to the cruelty and improper treatment of animals." In 1911 Parliament passed the Protection of Animals Act, which is still in effect today. The Protection of Animals Act was established on the principle that humans are free to dominate animals, but it is wrong to inflict unnecessary pain on them.

The movement in Great Britain to protect animal welfare quickly spread to other countries. In the United States the first anticruelty statute was enacted in New York in 1829; the law prohibited the malicious injuring or killing of farm animals. By 1907 every state had passed animal protection legislation, and by 1923 the laws also prohibited animal neglect and abandonment, cockfighting, and certain hunting traps. Congress passed the first federal law regarding the humane treatment of farm animals, the Humane Methods Slaughter Act, in 1958. The act required slaughterhouses to stun animals prior to killing them if their meat was to be sold to the federal government. This requirement soon became the standard by which all food animals were slaughtered. In 1966 Congress passed the Laboratory Animal Welfare Act, which regulated the care and treatment of animals other than rodents used in research experiments. Zoo and circus animals were added to the act in 1970 and 1976, respectively. New regulations concerning the treatment of animals in research labs were passed in 1985 after an activist from the animal rights group People for the Ethical Treatment of Animals (PETA), who was working undercover at a research lab, released a videotape of monkeys being mistreated. The new regulations included the mandatory use of painkillers for research animals and animal care training for personnel who work with animals, among other requirements.

PETA is just one of scores of animal rights groups that formed during the nineteenth and twentieth centuries. Other groups include the American Society for the Prevention of Cruelty to Animals (ASPCA), the Humane Society of the United States (HSUS), the Animal Welfare Institute (AWI), the International Society for Animal Rights (ISAR), the Animal Protection Institute (API), and the Fund for Animals (FFA), among others. Each organization represents a different philosophy on how animals should be treated and what legislation is necessary to protect them. Some organizations are moderate and advocate human use of animals as long as people do not inflict unnecessary pain on the animals. At the other end of the spectrum, some organizations, such as PETA, contend that all human use of animals is unethical and should be abolished. These varying philosophies are typically categorized as animal protection, or animal welfare, and animal rights.

According to agricultural policy professor Harold D. Guither, animal protection refers to "all efforts to prevent cruelty, improve humane treatment, reduce stress and strain, and monitor research with animals." People who believe in animal protection typically approve of raising animals for human consumption and animal use in research as long as the animals are treated humanely. Animal protectionists include activists who are driven by concern for the animals' welfare and people who profit from the human use of animals. Farmers, for example, frequently support animal protection measures because they believe that animals raised under humane conditions will be more productive and profitable. Animal protection and animal welfare philosophies correspond to traditional anticruelty efforts, such as legislation enacted in the nineteenth and early twentieth centuries.

Animal welfare and animal protection activists typically strive to raise public awareness about how animals are treated in agricultural, medical, and other industries. They usually oppose what they consider unnecessary uses of animals, such as killing minks for fur, and work to reduce the suffering of animals used for food and animal experimentation. Many of these supporters advocate the principle of the "three Rs"—replacement, reduction, and refinement. The three Rs typically refer to animal experimentation, but the concept can be extrapolated to other fields exploiting animals. Replacement means replacing techniques using animals with nonanimal techniques whenever possible. Substituting live animals in labs with artificially produced tissue cultures, or replacing mink or fox fur coats with fake fur coats are examples of replacement. Reduction refers to minimizing the numbers of animals used for a particular purpose. According to Guither, "Most toxicologists now agree that it is not necessary to use from sixty to two hundred rodents to generate a statistically precise lethal dose when perfectly adequate lethal dose data can be obtained using ten to twenty animals." Refinement refers to modifying the amount of pain and distress that is inflicted on an animal through human use. One example of refinement is revising slaughterhouse methods to reduce the trauma suffered by the animal being killed.

Animal rights (or animal liberation) philosophy, introduced in 1975 with Peter Singer's landmark book *Animal Liberation*, is a radical departure from the traditional animal welfare movement. In *Animal Liberation*, Singer argues that nonhuman animals, as sentient beings, have fundamental and inalienable rights that humans must not violate. Singer maintains that animals have the same rights as humans with similar mental capacities. For example, Singer contends that an "animal experiment cannot be justifiable unless the experiment is so important that the use of a brain-damaged human would be justifiable." According to Singer, animals and humans with comparable mental faculties should be treated equally because they both experience pain. In Singer's opinion, "All arguments to prove man's superiority cannot shatter this hard fact: In suffering the animals are our equals."

Singer and other animal rights philosophers differ radically from animal welfare pioneers such as Bentham, who argued that humans should not inflict unnecessary pain on animals. In contrast, animal rights activists believe that animals have a fundamental right not to be used for any human purpose, including medical experimentation, food, clothing, or entertainment. Considered the most radical of all animal advocates, many animal rights supporters, such as PETA, advocate the elimination of all uses of animals for food, clothing, amusement, or research purposes. According to PETA's mission statement, "PETA operates under the simple principle that animals are not ours to eat, wear, experiment on, or use for entertainment."

Animal rights activists lie at the radical end of a wide spectrum of animal advocacy. Most animal advocates do not support the extreme measures promoted by animal rights activists. The majority of animal supporters acknowledge that people are far too dependent upon animals for food, clothing, and medical discoveries to consider abolishing all human use of animals. However, it is undisputed among animal advocates that animals are sentient beings who deserve to be treated humanely. How to reconcile human use of animals with animal welfare is at the heart of the issues discussed in *Rights of Animals: Current Controversies.* Throughout this anthology, authors discuss the various ways humans exploit animals and debate whether or not such uses are justified.

Chapter 1

# Do Animals Have Rights?

# Animal Rights: An Overview

**by Joseph Lubinski**

**About the author:** *Joseph Lubinski is a contributor to the Animal Legal and Historical Center, a project of the Michigan State University-Detroit College of Law to provide the public with information concerning the legal aspects of animal rights.*

Forty years ago, the national rights debate was discussed in racial terms. Not long after, it expanded to include notions of sex and gender. Today, arguably, its scope spans even further—past the bounds of humankind. In 1975, Peter Singer brought to light the new animal protectionist cause in *Animal Liberation.* Commonly associated with animal rights, the book actually represents a utilitarian approach—one that denies the rights of any species and instead lobbies for equal consideration. Nonetheless, the book's arrival marked the awakening of the animal rights cause on the national political scene. Over twenty-five years later, the issues raised in the book continue to stir controversy. Animal rights, though perhaps not among the issues at the forefront of domestic policy concerns, is now a legitimate topic for discussion; one that stirs strong opinions on both sides.

## Changing Picture of Animals

Moreover, Singer's book does more than simply mark the beginning of an era, it highlights a changing picture of animals and their place in a human world. In its denial of rights, it helps to define them. Certainly, societal concern for animals is nothing new. Before the United States had abolished slavery, Great Britain was home to the world's first animal protectionist organization—the Royal Society for the Prevention of Cruelty to Animals, established in 1824. Its American counterpart, commonly known as the ASPCA, was founded just a few years later. Such groups, in addition to more well-known organizations like the Humane Society and World Wildlife Fund, advocate a sort of traditional welfare theory for animal protection. These organizations represent what has

Joseph Lubinski, "Legal Overview of Animal Rights," www.animallaw.info, 2002. Copyright © 2002 by Animal Legal and Historical Center. Reproduced by permission.

come to be known as the animal welfarist position. Welfarists seek to prevent the unnecessary suffering of animals, but at base believe that humans can and should continue to exploit other animals. This view is represented in the many state anti-cruelty statutes across the country and in federal laws such as the Animal Welfare Act and Humane Methods of Slaughter Act.

Rights advocates, on the other hand, seek to do something more for animals, perhaps much more by some estimates. To these people, animals are not another natural resource to be used and exploited by humanity. Rather, they, like humans, have certain inalienable entitlements that serve as a check on the freedom of every other living being. Animals have the right not to be slaughtered for minimal human benefit, a right not to endure suffering for small medical advances. In this country today, a strong case can be made that there are no true animal rights laws in effect. One might argue, however, that the Endangered Species Act as originally enacted in 1973 was a rights law. Indeed, so strict was the law in its initial form that the construction of a massive dam was stopped by the United States Supreme Court because its completion would destroy the habitat of a single species—the snail darter.

***"To [animal rights advocates], animals are not another natural resource to be used and exploited by humanity."***

Other countries, however, do have some sort of animal rights legislation. New Zealand, for example, made national news several years ago when it enacted legislation granting certain fundamental rights to members of the Great Apes—humanity's closest genetic relatives. More recently, the German parliament added animal rights language into the nation's constitution, a provision acknowledging the country's respect for the basic rights of all living creatures.

## Philosophers and Activists

Rights advocates might be thought of as falling into two groups—the philosophers and the activists. The activists, people like Tom Regan, advocate ending animal experimentation for medical and educational research, a ban on the use of animals for entertainment (such as in circuses), and the abolition of factory farming. Such activists seek strong new legislation that affords real protection to animals. They seek to give animals standing in court so that the endangered species can, in effect, protect themselves from humans. Such activists also seek to change the balance between animals and people by removing nonhumans' property classification. If animals were legally liberated from their master, a unique individual under the law, things would have to change.

The philosophers, like Mary Midgley, on the other hand, attempt to first change the way we as humans perceive animals. Waging a war of words and ideals, such rights advocates ask whether a dog is more like a toaster or a child—a thing or a person—and whether your dog is really your dog. Language and phrasing, then, are important. A doe is not an "it." She is a deer, after all, and a female deer at that. Such a distinction between the activist and the philosopher is, of course, imperfect. Many rights advocates are some combination of both. Moreover, as when comparing welfarism with rights theory, skeptics don't see a meaningful distinction, as the end result is the same—advocating real rights for nonhumans.

## At the Expense of Humans

To skeptics of animal rights, however, the line between such new rights proposals and traditional welfare theory, or classes of rights proponents, are distinctions without a difference. Either way, animal advocates seek to extend greater protections to animals, protections that might come at the expense of humans. Indeed, such skeptics oppose increased animal protections not because of their dislike or distaste for the animal kingdom, but rather because they fear new animal protections inevitably mean harm to people. Medicine is where it is today because of animal experimentation. Animals in circuses, aquariums, and zoos provide endless joy to millions of children and adults alike. Moreover, meat is a staple of the American diet and leather is both a fashionable and functional material for apparel. Animals are also an important part of the American economy—thousands, perhaps millions of jobs are on the line if animal rights make significant headway. Finally, and perhaps most fundamentally to rights opponents, animals are different than people. Whether one views it from a religious, evolutionary, or self-aggrandized perspective, humans are better than animals.

In the end, the point is not to determine who is right in the rights debate. As with so many other political, social, and ethical issues, it is too simplistic to label one side correct and the other wrong. Rather, the point is to spread awareness that animal rights is an issue, a serious issue worthy of public discourse. Already, change is underway across America and abroad. Several countries now recognize, at least on paper, some form of animal rights. Several American communities have begun rethinking the legal labels they attach to animals and pet owners. The wisdom and limits of such change will become important points for debate. As such, information on the issues is critical.

# Animals Have Rights

**by Tom Regan**

**About the author:** *Tom Regan is a professor of philosophy at North Carolina State University in Raleigh, North Carolina.*

Many people resist the idea of animal rights. Some of the objections are raised by academic philosophers; for example, some question the cogency of attributing a unified, complicated psychology to animals who are unable to use a language. Other objections are the stuff of everyday incredulity; objections of this type are voiced not only by philosophers but also by skeptical members of the general public. . . .

## The Absurdity of Animal Rights

Some critics challenge the idea of animal rights head-on. If animals have rights, they contend, we will have to acknowledge their right to vote, marry, and file for divorce, all of which is absurd. Thus, animals have no rights.

Now, part of what is said is true: any view that entails that animals have the right to vote, marry, and file for divorce is absurd. Clearly, however, the rights view entails nothing of the sort. Different individuals do not have to have all of the same rights in order to have some of the same rights. An eight-month-old child, for example, does not have either the right to vote or the other rights enumerated in the objection. But this does not mean that the child lacks the right to be treated with respect. On the contrary, young children possess this right, at least according to the rights view. And since these children possess this right while lacking the rights mentioned in the objection, there is no reason to judge the status of animals differently. Animals need not have the right to vote, marry, or file for divorce, if they have the right to be treated with respect.

## No Reciprocity

Critics of animal rights sometimes maintain that animals cannot have rights because animals do not respect human rights. Again, part of this objection is correct: animals do not respect our rights. Indeed, animals (we have every good

Carl Cohen and Tom Regan, *The Animal Rights Debate*. Lanham, MD: Rowman & Littlefield Publishers, Inc., 2001. Copyright © 2001 by Rowman & Littlefield Publishers, Inc. All rights reserved. Reproduced by permission.

reason to believe) have no idea of what it even means to respect someone else's rights. However, this lack of understanding and its behavioral consequence (namely, the absence of animal behavior that exhibits respect for human rights) do not undermine attributing rights to animals.

Once again, the moral status of young children should serve to remind us of how unfounded the requirement of reciprocity is. We do not suppose that young children must first respect our rights before we are duty bound to respect theirs. Reciprocity is not required in their case. We have no nonarbitrary, nonprejudicial reason to demand that animals conform to a different standard.

## Line Drawing

"But where do you draw the line? How do you know exactly which animals are subjects-of-a-life (and thus have a right to be treated with respect) and which animals are not?" There is an honest, simple answer to these vexing questions: we do not know exactly where to draw the line. Consciousness, which is presupposed by those who are subject-of-a-life [author's phrasing for a conscious being], is one of life's great mysteries. Whether mental states are identical with brain states or not, we have massive evidence that our having any mental states at all presupposes our having an intact, functioning central nervous system and brain activity above the brain stem. Where exactly this physiological basis for consciousness emerges on the phylogenic scale, where exactly it disappears, no one can really know with certainty. But neither do we need to know this.

***"Different individuals do not have to have all of the same rights in order to have some of the same rights."***

We do not need to know exactly how tall a person must be to be tall, before we can know that [basketball player] Shaquille O'Neal is tall. We do not need to know exactly how old a person must be to be old, before we can know that Grandma Moses was old. Similarly, we do not need to know exactly where an animal must be located on the phylogenic scale to be a subject-of-a-life, before we can know that the animals who concern us—those who are raised to be eaten, those who are ranched or trapped for their fur, or those who are used as models of human disease, for example—are subjects-of-a-life. We do not need to know everything before we can know something. Our ignorance about how far down the phylogenic scale we should go before we say that consciousness vanishes should not prevent us from saying where it is obviously present.

## Other Animals Eat Other Animals

Sometimes an objection to animal rights addresses a particular practice, such as meat eating. Critics point out that lions eat gazelles, after all, and then ask how it can be wrong if we eat steak. The most obvious difference in the two cases is that lions *have* to eat other animals to survive. We do not. So what a lion *must* do does not logically translate into what we *may* do.

Besides, it is worth noting how much this kind of objection diverges from our normal practice. Most Americans live in houses that have central heating and indoor plumbing, drive cars, wear clothes, and write checks. Other animals do not do any of these things. Should we therefore stop living as we live, stop doing what we do, and start imitating them? I know of no critic of animal rights who advocates anything remotely like this. Why, then, place what carnivorous animals eat in a unique category as being the one thing they do that we should imitate?

## Only Humans Are Inherently Valuable

Other objections to animal rights take different forms. For example, some critics maintain that because all and only human beings have inherent value, all and only human beings have a right to be treated with respect. How might this view be defended? Shall we say that all and only humans have the same level of intelligence, or autonomy, or reason? But there are many humans who lack these capacities and yet who, according to the rights view, have value above and beyond their possible usefulness to others. Will it then be suggested that this is true only in the case of human beings because only humans belong to the right species, the species *Homo sapiens*? But this is blatant speciesism [discrimination on the basis of species].

## Animals Have Less Inherent Value

Some critics contend that while animals have some inherent value, they have less, even far less, than we do. Attempts to defend this view can be shown to lack rational justification. What could be the basis of our having more inherent value than animals? Their lack of reason, or autonomy, or intellect? Only if, as is true of moral elitists like Aristotle, we are willing to make the same judgment in the case of humans who are similarly deficient. But it is not true that human subjects-of-a-life who have significantly less mental ability than is normal therefore have less inherent value than we do. It is not true (at least it is not true according to the rights view) that these humans may be treated merely as means in cases where it would be wrong to treat more competent humans in the same way. Those humans who are less mentally endowed are not the natural slaves of those of us who, without our having done anything to deserve it, are more fortunate when it comes to our innate intelligence. That being so, we cannot rationally sustain the view that animals like these humans in the relevant respects have less inherent value. All who have inherent value have it equally, all who exist as subjects-of-a-life have the same morally significant value—whether they be human animals or not.

***"What could be the basis of our having more inherent value than animals?"***

## Only Humans Have Souls

Some people think that the crucial difference between humans and other animals is that we do, whereas they do not, have a soul. After all, we are the ones who are created "in the image of God"; *that* is why all humans have inherent value and why every nonhuman animal lacks value of this kind. Proponents of this view have their work cut out for them. I am myself not ill disposed to the proposition that there are immortal souls. Personally, I profoundly hope I have one. But I would not want to rest my position on a controversial issue like this one about inherent value, on the even more controversial question about who or what has an immortal soul. Rationally, it is better to resolve moral issues without making more controversial assumptions than are needed. The question of who has inherent value is such a question, one that is resolved more rationally by reference to the subject-of-a-life criterion, without the introduction of the idea of immoral souls, than by its use.

***"It is better to resolve moral issues without making more controversial assumptions than are needed."***

But suppose we grant, for the sake of argument, that every human has an immortal soul and that every other animal lacks one. Would this justify the way we treat animals? More specifically, would this justify using mice in LD50 tests [which determine the toxicity of a substance by how quickly it kills 50 percent of its test subjects] or raising calves after the fashion of the milk-fed veal trade? Certainly not. Indeed, if anything, the absence of a soul arguably makes such conduct even more reprehensible than it already is. For consider: If we have immortal souls, then however bad our earthly lives have been, however much suffering and personal tragedy we have had to endure, we at least can look forward to the prospect of having a joyful existence in the eternal hereafter. Not so a milk-fed veal calf or a mouse whose internal organs burst in response to heavy doses of paint stripper. Absent a soul, there can be no other life after this one that compensates them for their misery while on Earth. Denied the possibility of such compensation, which we are assuming all humans enjoy, the pain, loneliness, terror, and other evils these animals suffer are, if anything, arguably worse than those experienced by human beings. So, no, the soul argument will not serve the purposes of those seeking a justification of the tyranny humans exercise over other animals. Just the opposite.

## What About Plants?

Inherent value, according to the rights view, belongs equally to all those who are subjects-of-a-life. Whether it belongs to other forms of life, including plants, or even to rocks and rivers, ecosystems, and the biosphere, are questions the rights view leaves open for others to explore, noting only that the onus of proof will be on those who wish to attribute inherent value beyond subjects-of-a-life to offer a principled, nonarbitrary, nonprejudicial, and rational defense of doing so.

Wherever the truth might lie concerning these matters, the rights view's implications concerning the treatment of animals are unaffected. We do not need to know how many people are eligible to vote in the next presidential election before we can know whether we are. Why should we need to know whether plants and the biosphere are inherently valuable before we can know that animals are?

And we do know that the billions of animals that, in our culture, are routinely eaten, trapped, and used in laboratories, for example, are like us in being subjects-of-a-life. And since, to arrive at the best account of our duties to one another, we must recognize *our* equal inherent value and *our* equal right to be treated with respect, reason—not mere sentiment, not unexamined emotion, but reason—compels us to recognize *their* equal inherent value and *their* equal right to respectful treatment.

## The Magnitude of Evil

Whether the ways animals are treated by humans adds to the evil of the world depends not only on how they are treated but also on what their moral status is. Not surprisingly, the rights view represents the world as containing far more evil than it is customary to acknowledge. First, and most obviously, there is the evil associated with the ordinary, day-to-day treatment to which literally billions of animals are subjected. . . . If it is true, as has been argued, that these animals have a right to be treated with respect, then the massive, day-to-day invasion of their bodies, denial of their basic liberties, and destruction of their very lives suggest a magnitude of evil so vast that, like light-years in astronomy, it is all but incomprehensible.

But this is not the end of the matter. For the magnitude of evil is much greater than the sum of the violations of animal rights and the morally wrong assaults on their independent value these violations represent. Recall that one of the weaknesses of preference utilitarianism is that it cannot rule out counting evil preferences in the process of reaching a fully informed judgment of moral right and wrong. This is a weakness that any plausible moral outlook must remedy, and the rights view has a way of doing so. . . . According to the rights view evil preferences are those preferences which, if acted on, either lead agents to violate someone's rights or cause others to approve of, or tolerate, such violations.

> ***"Absent a soul, there can be no other life after this one that compensates [animals] for their misery while on Earth."***

From the perspective of the rights view, therefore, the magnitude of the evil in the world is not represented only by the evil done to animals when their rights are violated; it includes as well the innumerable human preferences that are satisfied by doing so. That the majority of people who act on such preferences (e.g., people who earn a living in the fur industry or those who frequent KFC) do not recognize the preferences that motivate them as evil—indeed, that some will adamantly assert that nothing could be further from the truth—settles nothing. Whether the preferences we act on are evil is not something to be established by asking how strenuously we deny that they are; their moral status depends on whether by acting on them we are party to or complicit in the violation of someone's rights.

Are all those who act on evil preferences evil people? Not at all. . . . People are evil (at least this is the clearest example of what we mean) when their general character leads them to habitually violate others' rights *and* to do so cruelly, either by taking pleasure in or by feeling nothing (being indifferent) about the suffering or loss caused by the violation. While some who benefit from animal rights' violations may meet this description, the majority of people, including those who, as part of their day-to-day life, are supportive or tolerant of this evil, are not. In the vast majority of cases, I believe, those associated with the meat industry, for example, and those who support it by acting on their gustatory preferences, are not evil people. And the same is true of the vast majority of other people who either are themselves actively engaged in industries that routinely violate the rights of animals or are supportive or complicit in these violations.

***"The magnitude of evil is much greater than the sum of the violations of animal rights and the morally wrong assaults on their independent value."***

The judgment that otherwise decent people act on evil preferences in these ways may invite anger and resentment from some, hoots of derisive laughter from others; but it may also awaken still others to a larger sense of the moral significance of our life, including (even) the moral significance of our most mundane choices: what we put in our mouths and wear on our backs. Imperfect creatures that we are, living in an imperfect world, no one of us can be entirely free from our role in the evil around us. That recognition of the rights of animals reveals far more evil than was previously suspected is no reason to deny the magnitude of the evil that exists in the world at large or how much, on close examination, we find in ourselves; rather, our common moral task is to conscientiously search for ways to lessen both.

# Discrimination on the Basis of Species Is Unjust

**by Marc Bekoff**

**About the author:** *Marc Bekoff is a professor in the Department of Environmental, Population, and Organismic Biology at the University of Colorado in Boulder.*

The issues with which those interested in nonhuman animal (hereafter "animal") protection must deal are numerous, diverse, difficult, and extremely contentious; interdisciplinary work is needed to try to come to terms with them. Matters of concern include which individuals or groups of animals should be the focus of moral concern, what criteria are most appropriate for making such decisions, what regulations are appropriate and how they should be enforced, and whether students should be required to engage in vivisection or dissection. Reasonable people with common interests in the protection of animals from human exploitation often disagree on basic issues and on where different points of view can take them.

## What Is Wrong with Speciesism

One of the most significant animal protection movements ever to arise with strong and ever-growing interdisciplinary support is The Great Ape Project (GAP). Its ambitious, important goal is to admit all great apes (including humans) to the Community of Equals, in which the following basic moral principles or rights, enforceable by law, are granted: the right to life, the protection of individual liberty, and the prohibition of torture. And the GAP is working. Indeed, the British government has recently announced a ban on the use of great apes in research, based mainly on their cognitive and behavioral characteristics.

Nevertheless, despite its ambitious goals and strong interdisciplinary support, the GAP is speciesist [discrimination on the basis of species] because of its greater concern with great apes over other animals. In the context of animal use, speciesists make decisions about how humans are permitted to treat other

Marc Bekoff, "Resisting Speciesism and Expanding the Community of Equals," *BioScience*, vol. 48, August 1998, p. 638. Copyright © 1998 by *BioScience*. Reproduced by permission of Copyright Clearance Center, Inc.

animals based on an individual's species membership (for example, all and only humans or all and only specific mammals might constitute protected groups) rather than on that animal's individual unique characteristics. Nonspeciesists, by contrast, use an individual's unique characteristics to make moral decisions about animal use and are concerned with how individual animals are viewed and treated. For example, J. Rachels's [author of *Created From Animals: The Moral Implications of Darwinism*] notion of moral individualism is based on the following argument "If A is to be treated differently from B, the justification must be in terms of A's individual characteristics and B's individual characteristics. Treating them differently cannot be justified by pointing out that one or the other is a member of some preferred group, not even the 'group' of human beings." According to this view, careful attention must be paid to individual variations in behavior within species.

Speciesists also often use such words as "higher" and "lower" to refer to different groups of animals. However, the use of such words, and activities such as ranking species by drawing lines to place different groups of animals "above" and "below" others, are misleading because they fail to take into account the lives and worlds of the animals themselves. Speciesism also can ignore evolutionary continuity. Nevertheless, use of such words is common. For example, a recent essay on animal use perpetuates the myth of there being "lower" and "higher" animals by referring to animals "lower on the phylogenetic tree." Furthermore, deciding which among the criteria that are used to place species in some hierarchical order are morally relevant and how these criteria are to be evaluated presents serious problems, even if one were able to argue convincingly that species should be ranked on a single scale.

In practice, when deciding about the types of treatment to which animals will be exposed, speciesism is often used narrowly, to mean "primatocentrism" or "humanism," and human superiority is often implied in speciesist arguments. However, individuals representing many other species experience pain, anxiety, and suffering (physically and psychologically), even if these are not the same sorts of pain, anxiety, and suffering that are experienced by humans, or even other animals, including members of the same species. Although practical considerations made it important to start somewhere in the attempt to recognize the rights of nonhumans, I believe that it is time to make a serious effort to broaden the GAP to The Great Ape/Animal Project (GA/AP) and to expand membership in the community of equals. In the GA/AP it will be presupposed that all individual animals should be included in the community of equals and be granted the right to life, the protection of individual liberty, and the prohibition of torture. Humans have a prima facie (all other things being equal) obligation to grant moral standing to all animals, not only sentient beings, and this starting point will require the

***"The [Great Ape Project] is speciesist."***

rights of all animals to be respected when moral decisions are being made about overriding these rights. All life would be revered.

## Speciesist Cognitivism: Difficult Moral Dilemmas

Speciesists often appeal to cognitive differences in species-typical behavior and interspecific variations in "intelligence" when making decisions about animal use. For example, people often ask whether "lower" animals, such as fish or dogs, are able to perform sophisticated patterns of behavior that are usually associated with "higher" animals, such as nonhuman primates. This question commonly takes the form of "Do dogs ape?" or "Do fish dog?" In my view, these questions are misguided because individuals have to be able to do what they need to do in order to live in their own worlds.

Although there are species differences in behavior, behavioral differences in and of themselves may mean little for arguments about animal protection. Indeed, it is to be expected that species differences in behavior will be the rule rather than the exception, but these variations should not be viewed as being "good" or "bad" or used to place animals "higher" or "lower" on a linear scale. Thus, narrow-minded primatocentric and humanocentric speciesist cognitivism must be resisted in studies of animal cognition and in the application of knowledge in this area to decisions about how animals should be treated. Nonetheless, some researchers write as if only some nonhuman primates, especially the great apes, along with human primates, have rich cognitive lives. For example, consider Richard Byrne's claims in his excellent book, *The Thinking Ape*:

***"Human superiority is often implied in speciesist arguments."***

> It seems that the great apes, especially the common chimpanzee, can attribute mental states to other individuals; but no other group of animals can do so—apart from ourselves, and perhaps cetaceans. This contrasts with the findings on understanding of beliefs, attribution of intentions, and how things work—where a sharp discontinuity is implied between great apes and all other animals.
>
> Of course, until similar painstaking work is done with monkeys, we cannot argue that only apes have such abilities . . . and no-one has yet risked the huge expenditure of time and money to find out.

Primatocentric claims are based on very few comparative data derived from tests on very small numbers of nonhuman primates who might not be entirely representative of their species. The range of tests that have been used to obtain evidence of intentional attributions is also extremely small, and such tests are often biased toward activities that may favor apes over monkeys or members of other, nonprimate species. Furthermore, much of the work that has been done on nonhuman primates has involved only a few of the many extant species. [More than fifteen] years ago, B.B. Beck [author of *Chimpocentrism: Bias In Cognitive Ethology*] warned about the dangers of chimpocentrism in studies of animal cognition. More recently, M. Tomasello and J. Call [in *Primate Cognition*] concluded that "the experimental foundation for claims that apes are 'more intelligent' than monkeys is not a solid one, and there are few if any naturalistic observations that would substantiate such broad-based, species-general claims."

## Nonprimates

Turning to nonprimates, more data need to be collected and existing data reevaluated before the possibility is dismissed that at least some nonprimate individuals also have rich cognitive lives. Byrne clearly qualifies his generalizations and admits that the necessary broad comparative research has not yet been conducted. In a review of social cognition in nonhuman primates and birds, P. Marler writes [in *Social Cognition: Are Primates Smarter Than Birds?*]: "I am driven to conclude, at least provisionally, that there are more similarities than differences between birds and primates." Although he was concerned with groups of animals and not individuals, certainly the behavior patterns that are used to characterize families or species, for example, are those performed by individuals. Other students of behavior have also recognized that cross-species comparisons often result in attributing cognitive abilities to individuals of species that are frequently excluded in discussions of animal cognition.

Researchers are clearly a long way from having an adequate database from which meaningful claims about the taxonomic distribution of various cognitive skills can emerge. Nevertheless, it is still possible to discuss whether chimps are "smarter" than, for example, mice or dogs. However, researchers must be clear about why they might feel comfortable with the claim that chimps are on average smarter than mice. That is, they need to be clear about the criteria that are used to make comparative statements about smartness and intelligence—what they mean when and if they claim that chimps' social lives are more complex than those of mice, that chimps are able to solve more complex or difficult problems, or that chimps show more versatile patterns of behavior in response to environmental changes. And it is important to remember that mice and chimps do well in their own worlds, and that neither would do well in the other's. The main point is that although most people would probably not have much trouble deciding to harm or to kill a mouse rather than a chimp if they were forced to make a choice, this decision should not be made summarily or conveniently along species lines.

> ***"Drawing moral boundaries at the species level . . . is fraught with difficulties."***

Drawing moral boundaries at the species level using some set of average species-typical characteristics is fraught with difficulties. Indeed, in some instances (for example, when considering whether to use a healthy mouse rather than a severely mentally impaired chimp in a persistent vegetative state in an experiment, or debating restraining the physical movements of a healthy mouse rather than of a severely physically disabled chimp), it might be argued that an individual mouse rather than an individual chimp should be spared. But in decisions such as these, it is not necessary that a normal mouse be compared with an abnormal chimp. For example, if it were the case that some procedure could be carried out harmlessly on a chimp but would require harming a mouse, then the mouse should be spared. Such thought experiments would force people to come to terms with difficult issues on a case-by-case basis and not merely hand wave that chimps should always be spared.

## Deepening Ethology and Doing Science

> At that point I was working with squid, and I think squid are the most beautiful animals in the world. And it just began to bother me. I began to have the feeling that nothing I could find out was worth killing another squid. (Ruth Hubbard, as quoted by M. Holloway [in *Profile—Ruth Hubbard: Turning the Inside Out*].)

Studying nonhuman animals is a privilege that must not be abused. Researchers must take this privilege seriously and respect the dignity of the animals whom they use. Scientists who compassionately express their feelings about the pain and suffering that is brought to many animals and who question how science is done are acting responsibly despite the risks to their careers; they are not traitors or turncoats. Questioning science makes for better, more responsible science, and questioning the ways in which humans use animals will make for more informed decisions about animal use. One way to accomplish this goal is to teach children and students to make responsible decisions about animal use in the face of peer or other pressure to conform to historical precedent. As J. Mench has noted [in *Animal Research Arouses Passion, Sparks Debate*]: "Science no longer occupies the privileged and unassailable position that it once did. People increasingly question the benefits of 'progress' in extending life, engineering the human and animal genome, and developing new reproductive and biomedical technologies. Science, moreover, is largely a publicly funded activity. Appropriately, accountability is the new watchword, and public education and consensus-building are the new goals." Indeed, much research is being done to develop alternatives to animal use, especially in scientific research.

> ***"Studying nonhuman animals is a privilege that must not be abused."***

The enterprise of science might also benefit if researchers who use animals showed more sensitivity to the animals they use. Although J.B. Poole has maintained [in *Happy Animals Make Good Science*] that "happy animals make good science" (essentially because they are less stressed), it is important to remember that if individuals have the capacity to be happy then they also have the capacity to be sad and, most certainly, the ability to feel pain and to suffer. Furthermore, some researchers (taking a nonspeciesist view) show different attitudes toward animals of the same species depending on the context in which they are used—that is, whether they are encountered in the laboratory or at home. Many scientists who name, bond with, and praise the cognitive abilities of the companion animals (for example, dogs) with whom they share their homes are likely to leave this sort of "baggage" at home when they enter their laboratories to do research with other members of the same species. Based on a series of interviews with practicing scientists, M.T. Phillips reported [in *Proper Names and the Construction of Biography: The Negative Case of Laboratory Animals*] that many of them construct a distinct category of animal, the 'laboratory animal,' that contrasts with namable animals (e.g., pets) across every salient dimension . . . the cat or dog in the laboratory is perceived by researchers as ontologically different from the pet dog or cat at home." In other words, the laboratory animal is treated as an object rather than a subject. A. Rowan has noted [in *Scientists and Animal Research*] that perhaps if scientists were less coldly objective about their research and showed even a little compassion for the nonhumans whom they use, then those who question science in general, and the use of animals in particular, might be more sympathetic to the use of some animals in some research.

***"The laboratory animal is treated as an object rather than a subject."***

With respect to possible links between the study of animal cognition and the protection of innocent, nonconsenting animals, I believe that "deep ethology" will help people to become more aware of their moral and ethical obligations to all animals. I use the term "deep ethology" to stress that humans not only are an integral part of nature but also have unique responsibilities to nature. Those who appeal to the "brutality of nature" to justify some humans' treatment of animals fail to see that animals are not moral agents. Rather, animals are moral patients in that they cannot be held responsible (as are most human beings as moral agents) for their actions as being "right" or "wrong" or "good" or "bad." Indeed, if viewing animals as moral agents attributes to them cognitive abilities that are correlated with the ability to make moral judgments, the possession of such abilities would make animal use even more objectionable.

Deep ethology also means being sensitive to the worlds of animals themselves and making serious attempts to adopt their points of view. Humans can learn a lot about our nonhuman kin if we carefully observe and listen to them. When all individual animals are admitted to the community of equals, they will be protected regardless of their cognitive skills or their capacities to experience pain, anxiety, and suffering. Overriding their rights would then require serious debate.

*Chapter 1*

## Giving Animals the Benefit of the Doubt

Even within the confines of moral individualism, decisions about how individuals may be used are extremely difficult. As A. Linzey has stressed [in *Sentientism*], as humans' own moral sensibilities develop and our scientific understanding increases, moral distinctions are likely to change as well. I have argued that when we are unsure about an individual's ability to reason or to think, then we should assume that he or she can do so, in his or her ways. And when we are uncertain about an individual's ability to experience pain, anxiety, and suffering, then we must assume that he or she can do so. We should err on the side of the animals. In the end, it really is the compromising of other lives that needs to be dealt with in a serious manner, regardless of whether individuals are smart or are able to feel pain and to suffer physically or psychologically.

To sum up, "we" versus "them" dualisms just do not work—not in speciesist views of "animals" versus "humans," and not when opponents in debates about animal use portray one another in this manner. It is the similarities rather than the differences between humans and other animals that drives much research in which animals' lives are compromised. If "they" who are used in research are so much like "us," then much more work needs to be done to justify certain research practices. Humans need to appreciate our common moral status and enter into intimate and reciprocal relationships with all beings in this more-than-human world.

# The Legal Rights of Great Apes Should Be Recognized

**by Steven M. Wise**

**About the author:** *Steven M. Wise has practiced animal protection law for over twenty years and teaches animal-rights law at the Harvard Law School, Vermont Law School, and John Marshall Law School. He is the founder and president of the Center for the Expansion of Fundamental Rights, Inc., and is the former president of the Animal Legal Defense Fund.*

I will not argue that any chimpanzee or bonobo has full autonomy. But no bright line divides full autonomy from realistic autonomy or realistic autonomy from the legal fiction that "all humans are autonomous." However, a little mountain geography might help us understand the relationships among them a little better. We'll start at the top of the world. The summit of 29,038-foot Mount Everest in the Himalayas will represent those few humans who may have attained full autonomy. A few more occupy the apex of K-2 in the Karakoram Range in northern Kashmir, which at 28,250 feet is the second-highest mountain in the world. Millions cluster atop the highest mountain in the Hindu Kush Range, 25,260-foot Tirich Mir, located in Pakistan along the Afghan border. The nearby Pamir Range in Tajikistan is filled with peaks above 20,000 feet. The autonomies of most adult *Homo erectus*, Neandertals, and *Homo sapiens* can be found among those peaks.

Sea level represents autonomy's absence. The top of Cadillac Mountain, jutting 1,530 feet from the Atlantic on the eastern side of Mt. Desert Island, Maine, stands for the minimum autonomy that judges require to trigger human dignity and entitle one to dignity-rights, unaided by any legal fiction. We'll let 250-foot Flying Mountain, on Mt. Desert Island's west side, stand for the highest autonomy that Aristotle and the ancient Stoics believed nonhuman animals, whom they thought could only perceive and act on impulse, ever attained.

Steven M. Wise, *Rattling the Cage: Toward Legal Rights for Animals*. Cambridge, MA: Perseus Books, 2000. Copyright © 2000 by Steven M. Wise. All rights reserved. Reproduced by permission.

The autonomies of the Language Research Center's [at Georgia State University] four adult apes [Kanzi, Panbanisha, Sherman and Tamuli] tower above Cadillac Mountain. If a phalanx of primatologists is right, we can place the autonomy of mother-raised [chimpanzee] Tamuli, who has a complex cognition but lacks the ability to use symbols, at the tip of Mount Etna, which rises 10,902 feet above Sicily. If [professor] Juan Carlos Gómez is correct, hand-reared but languageless [chimpanzee] Sherman, who has all Tamuli's cognitive abilities and uses symbols to boot and has an implicit theory of mind and implicit self-consciousness, can be symbolized by Mt. Blanc, which at 15,771 feet is the highest Alp. If [primatologists] Sue Savage-Rumbaugh, Michael Tomasello, Roger Fouts, and others are correct, human-enculturated [bonobos] Kanzi and Panbanisha have all Sherman's cognitive abilities but also possess at least some, and perhaps all, the elements needed for an explicit theory of mind, comprehend human language at the level of at least a three-year-old human, produce language like a human two-year-old, are explicitly self-conscious, and demonstrate a raft of other complicated cognitive abilities. Their autonomies may not top the 20,000-foot level, as do most human adults with advanced language abilities, complex consciousnesses and theories of mind, and numerous other highly advanced cognitive abilities. But they reach the pinnacle of Mt. Kilimanjaro, which at 19,340 feet is the tallest African mountain.

> ***"No bright line divides full autonomy from realistic autonomy."***

Today, the autonomy of [bonobo] Nyota, at just one year old, probably lies just shy of Cadillac Mountain's peak. But early reports suggest that his cognition is advancing so rapidly that his may be the first nonhuman autonomy to reach the height of Mt. McKinley, which at 20,320 feet is the highest peak in North America. At birth, my daughter Siena's autonomy floated just about at sea level. So did those of Kanzi, Panbanisha, Sherman, Tamuli, and Nyota. As did they, Siena vaulted past 250-foot Flying Mountain early in her first year. Kanzi, Panbanisha, Sherman, and Tamuli all topped 1, 530-foot Cadillac Mountain late in their first year or perhaps early in their second, and Siena and Nyota probably will, too, and on just about the same schedule. But now Siena will begin to accelerate. Sometime in the second half of her second year or perhaps early in her third year, she will race past Tamuli and overtake Sherman. If she continues to develop normally, by age four, or by age five at the latest, she will overhaul Kanzi and Panbanisha, then spend the rest of her life slowly ascending toward Everest, probably never reaching it. Nyota's probable course of development is less well-known.

## Present or Potential Autonomy

Notice how I used "probably," "likely," "if she continues to develop normally," and "probable course of development" in describing Nyota's and

Siena's future autonomies. They may not advance an inch—who can know? In determining entitlement to dignity-rights, should one look to a being's *present* or *potential* autonomy? At one extreme, [philosopher] H. Tristam Englehardt Jr. argues that the nature of rights demands that entitlement be determined at the time the question "Do you have a right?" is asked. He says flatly that "if X is a potential Y, it follows that X is not a Y. If fetuses are potential persons, it follows clearly that fetuses are not persons. As a consequence, X does not have the actual rights of Y, but only potentially the rights of Y." At the other extreme, the philosopher John Rawls argues that one with a potential should have full rights, whether or not one's capacities have been developed. Between these poles lie a host of other arguments.

We need not decide the question. Under the common law, autonomy determines entitlement to dignity, and legal personhood. The evidence is strong that normal humans, chimpanzees, and bonobos all reach Cadillac Mountain's height (the minimum necessary autonomy to trigger dignity) by the end of their first or the beginning of their second year. If we accept the argument for potential autonomy, then both bonobo and child are entitled to dignity-rights. If we reject it, then neither is *entitled* to dignity-rights. Whether one or both gets them will turn on the willingness of judges to use a legal fiction that one or both is autonomous until they actually become so. If judges choose the usual "all humans are autonomous" fiction to extend dignity-rights to Siena alone, Nyota will have no argument that as a matter of *liberty*, he is being treated unjustly. As we will see, equality will be another matter altogether.

***"Under common law, autonomy determines entitlement to dignity and legal personhood."***

## Similar Autonomies

In 1988, [chimpanzee] Jerom, infected with two strains of HIV, was languishing in the small, windowless, cinder-block cell within the Yerkes Regional Primate Research Center. He had eight more pain-wracked years to live. That year, Yerkes' director, Frederick King, coauthored an article, "Primates," with three Yerkes colleagues in the prestigious journal *Science.* His justification of routine invasions of the bodily liberties and bodily integrities of primates on the ground of their *similarity to humans* is shocking stuff to those who value equality.

> [S]imilarities in the biological mechanisms of humans and primates underlie the value of these animals for research in a broad range of disciplines . . .
>
> Primates have played a major role in increasing our knowledge of the structure, organization, chemistry, and physiology of the human brain. The complexity of the primate brain and its similarity to that of humans makes *[sic]* primates excellent subjects for the study of motivational states such as hunger, thirst, and emotion. . . .

> The large, convoluted cerebral cortex, with great areas devoted to associational activities, is almost certainly responsible for the primate's ability to learn highly complex cognitive tasks beyond the capacities of species other than humans.
>
> Because the primate brain shares with humans a high degree of plasticity, their cognitive and social behaviors are heavily dependent on learning and the environment, as is the human behavioral repertoire. Hence in studies of the relationship of neural plasticity and the emergence of behaviors dependent upon social learning primates are often the subject of choice. . . .
>
> [P]rimates in general develop socially and relate to each other and their environments in ways that are more similar to humans than to other animals.

King concluded by noting that the animal-rights activists' "campaign against primate research is actually based on the scientists' rationale for studying primates: the biological and behavioral similarities of primates to humans.". . .

King believes that all rights are bestowed by human beings. Here he fails to grasp that equality destroyed anywhere, even for chimpanzees, threatens the destruction of equality everywhere. That is why, near the onset of the American Civil War, Abraham Lincoln told Congress that "[i]n giving freedom to the slave, we assure freedom to the free." To deny freedom to the slave, the Confederacy had to shackle its white citizens. Had Pickett's Charge split the Union lines at Gettysburg, the American South might today be dotted with biomedical research laboratories using not just slaves, instead of nonhuman primates, but anyone that the government, like King, thought most useful.

King's unembarrassed advocacy, in one of the world's most respected scientific journals, of using raw power to exploit nonhuman primates *because they are like us* rests on an argument that is arbitrary, unprincipled, and corrosive to equality, which at bottom demands that likes be treated alike. The equality rights of chimpanzees and bonobos must be determined by comparing them to others who already have rights. If alikes are treated differently or if unalikes are treated the same, for no good and sufficient reason, equality is violated. The following three equality arguments all lead to the same conclusion: King was wrong, at least with respect to chimpanzees and bonobos.

***"Equality destroyed anywhere . . . threatens the destruction of equality everywhere."***

## Three Arguments for Equality

The first of three equality arguments that we can present in court will be this: Kanzi, Panbanisha, Sherman, Tamuli, and Nyota are entitled to the rights to bodily integrity and bodily liberty *if* humans with similar autonomies are entitled to them. The second argument will be: Kanzi, Panbanisha, Sherman, Tamuli, and Nyota's autonomies entitle them to bodily integrity and bodily liberty *if* humans who completely lack autonomy have their rights. The third argument: If the autonomies of any of the five chimpanzees and bonobos are insufficient to entitle them to the rights to bodily integrity and bodily liberty in full, they are still entitled to them in proportion to the degree to which their autonomies approach the necessary minimum *if* humans with similar autonomies are entitled to these rights in proportion to the degree to which *their* autonomies approach the necessary minimum. In each argument, we will compare chimpanzees and bonobos to a different class of humans who possess the fundamental rights to bodily integrity and bodily liberty.

***"Each person should be treated as an individual rather than as a statistic."***

Few would argue that the complex autonomies of chimpanzees and bonobos would not entitle them to bodily liberty and bodily integrity if they were human. We have seen that they are not disqualified from these rights as *liberties* because they are not human. The strongest assault against ape equality has been mounted by the philosopher Carl Cohen. "The issue," Cohen says, "is one of kind." Sure, Cohen says, some humans lack autonomy. But others are as fully autonomous as [philosopher Immanuel] Kant could ever have dreamed. Cohen argues that their full autonomies should therefore be imputed to every human, regardless of actual ability. But Cohen's argument is illogical. The species *Homo sapiens* cannot rationally be designated as the boundary of any relevant "kind" that includes every fully autonomous human. Other "kinds" exist. Some categories are broader, for example, those of animals, vertebrates, mammals, primates, and apes. At least one "kind" is narrower, that of normal adult humans, which also contains every fully autonomous human.

Cohen's argument for group benefits is not just logically but morally flawed. The philosopher James Rachels has pointed out how it "assumes that we should determine how an individual is to be treated, not on the basis of *its* qualities but on the basis of *other* individual's qualities." You get straight As; I go to Harvard. I jump thirty feet; you go to the Olympics. You look like Elle MacPherson; I get a modeling contract. Unsurprisingly, many people are bothered by this kind of argument. Surprisingly, Cohen is one of them. He has attacked racial affirmative-action policies as "illegal and immoral" because they favor blacks over whites in precisely the way he favors humans over apes. But even Harvard Law School professor Laurence Tribe, who supports racial and sexual affirmative action, has acknowledged the "tenaciously held principle . . . with undeniable constitutional roots . . . that each person should be treated as an individual rather than as a statistic or as a member of a group—particularly of a group the individual did not knowingly choose to join."

## Group Benefits

This does not mean that racial or sexual affirmative action is always wrong or should be illegal. Something like Cohen's notion of group benefits is occasionally used to *correct* the effects of prior discrimination in the United States. But even then, judges often manifest what Tribe called a "considerable unease" in sharply divided endorsements of affirmative action plans. Judges are not alone. In a *New York Times*-CBS poll taken at the end of 1997, 25 percent of Americans said they wished to abolish affirmative-action programs outright, 43 percent wanted them changed, and just 24 percent would leave them as they are.

A 1996 case, *Hopwood v. State of Texas*, exemplifies the rising judicial resistance to the use of affirmative action for reasons other than to correct past discrimination. There, the Fifth Circuit Court of Appeals flatly barred the use of race as a factor in university admissions to achieve the goal of a diverse student body. Affirmative action, it said,

> treats minorities as a group, rather than as individuals. . . . The assumption is that a certain individual possesses characteristics by virtue of being a member of a certain racial group. This assumption, however, does not withstand scrutiny. The use of a racial characteristic to establish a presumption that the individual also possesses other, and socially relevant, characteristics exemplifies, encourages, and legitimizes the mode of thought and behavior that underlies most prejudice and bigotry in modern America.

Group benefits stir intense controversy even in racial affirmative-action plans that are anchored in the laudable desire to correct ancient discrimination and achieve racial equality for a long-oppressed minority. But outside of apartheid-era South Africa or Nazi Germany, group benefits have never been used in the way that Cohen and others would use it against apes, as a sword instead of a shield.

## Greater Autonomies

Some humans—infants, young children, the anencephalic (who suffer from the congenital absence of major portions of the skull, scalp, and brain, never attain consciousness, can neither feel nor suffer, and usually die within a few months of birth), the severely mentally retarded, and those in persistent vegetative states—either lack autonomy or have autonomies too "low" to be called "realistic" (falling below the peak of Cadillac Mountain). Judges routinely award them dignity-rights anyway by using the "all humans are autonomous" legal fiction. But if judges recognize the liberties of these humans but reject the liberties of apes with *greater* autonomy, they act perversely, and their decisions cannot be explained except as acts of naked prejudice. Of course, it is always open to judges to sever autonomy from dignity. But only a foolish hydroelectric-plant manager would stem flooding in the control room by diverting the river that generates the electricity.

> ***"If judges recognize the liberties of . . . humans but reject the liberties of apes . . . they act perversely."***

The lowest autonomy of any adult ape, Tamuli's, lies at the level of 10,902-

feet Mount Etna. I won't argue, here, that equality entitles nonhuman animals whose autonomies exist at the level of 1,530-foot Cadillac Mountain or even at the height of 3,491-foot Mt. Greylock, highest of the Berkshires, to any fundamental right, though compelling arguments can be made. I will leave it at this: At some point the disparity between the autonomies of nonhuman animals with *no legal rights* and the virtual sea-level autonomies of humans *with* dignity-rights becomes completely indefensible.

***"Courts strain to give even the most severely disabled humans 'some measure of personal control over their lives'."***

I said that if *potential* autonomy was insufficient to justify an entitlement to dignity-rights, the immunities of both my infant daughter, Siena, and Nyota would turn on the sufferance of judges until their autonomies rose to the level of Cadillac Mountain. I also conceded that if judges extended these rights to bodily integrity and bodily liberty just to Siena, not because they were her due but as a gift, Nyota would have no claim that as a matter of liberty, he was being treated unjustly. But the situation is different with equality. Neither Siena nor Nyota are autonomous now; both have only the potential for autonomy. If Siena's potential for achieving an autonomy peak in the mid-to-high 20,000-foot range is ignored, Nyota has no equality claim to the recognition of his potential for achieving an autonomy peak in the low 20,000-foot range. But if Siena's potentiality is sufficient for giving her fundamental rights, Nyota's potential must equally be recognized.

## Proportional Autonomies

Humans infants, young children, and the severely mentally retarded or autistic who lack the autonomy necessary to entitle them to full liberty rights are not totally denied them. Judges give them dignity-rights, and even the right to choose, by using the legal fiction that "all humans are autonomous." However, as their autonomies *approach* the minimum, the *scope* of their fundamental rights may be varied *proportionately.* If so, equality demands that the rights of animals who possess the same degree of autonomy as these humans possess vary proportionately, too. . . .

"Proportionality rights" can vary in three dimensions. First, humans who lack sufficient autonomy may be allowed *fewer* legal rights than autonomous humans. But judges do not characterize them as legal things. For example, their right to engage in a political process that they cannot understand might be restricted by refusing them the right to vote. But we cannot vivisect them. Severely developmentally disabled humans cannot testify in a court, but we do not enslave them. To the contrary, courts strain to give even the most severely disabled humans "some measure of personal control over their lives" in an effort to "maximize the personal autonomy and dignity" along with conditions of reasonable care and safety and a reasonably nonrestrictive environment. To the extent that any of the Language Research Center apes that Savage-Rumbaugh wants me to help her return home lack the autonomy necessary to entitle them to liberty rights in full, they should be given *fewer* rights than one whose autonomy is sufficient, *if* humans who lack minimum autonomy are given these rights. They are not to be reduced to legal things, enslaved, or vivisected. Equality requires that they be given the same rights to "maximize the personal autonomy and dignity" that they possess. If the rights of apes must be restricted—and in America they must—they are also entitled to live in similar conditions of reasonable care and safety and in a reasonable nonrestrictive environment.

Second, judges may *narrow* the liberty rights of humans who lack minimum autonomy. Their right to bodily liberty may be restricted so that they can exercise it only in a manner consistent with both public and their own safety. That is why state institutions for the mentally retarded may physically restrain the movements of their dangerous residents and parents can commit children to a state institution without an adversary proceeding. But these patients are not reduced to legal things then enslaved or vivisected. To the extent that any of the Language Research Center apes lack the autonomy necessary to entitle them to liberty rights in full, they should be given *narrower* rights than one whose autonomy is sufficient, *if* humans who lack minimum autonomy are given these rights. Their right to bodily liberty might be restricted in a manner consistent with the public safety and their own safety. But they are not to be reduced to legal things, enslaved, or vivisected.

Third, courts and legislatures might give humans who lack minimum autonomy *partial elements* of a complex right. Remember that most of what we normally think of as legal rights are actually a bundle of rights. My legal right to bodily integrity means that I have the negative liberty-right that you not hit me, an immunity-right that disables you from legally hitting me, a claim-right against you if you do hit me, a power-right to sue you in a court, and more. Humans whose autonomies fall below the necessary minimum are sometimes given all these rights, but not the power-right to waive them, because they can't understand what it means to waive their rights. Thus, an adult woman in a permanent vegetative state might lack the right to refuse life-saving medical treatment and a twelve-year-old boy might lack the right to waive his right to remain silent when accused of crime. But neither the woman nor the boy is reduced to a legal thing and enslaved or vivisected. To the extent that any of the Language Research Center apes lack the autonomy necessary to entitle them to liberty rights in full, they are entitled to partial elements of a complex right, *if* humans who lack minimum autonomy are given them. They are not to be reduced to legal things, enslaved, or vivisected.

# Animals Do Not Have Rights

**by David S. Oderberg**

**About the author:** *David S. Oderberg is the Reader in Philosophy at the University of Reading, England. This viewpoint draws on material from his book* Applied Ethics, *in which his argument against animal rights is set out in detail.*

The animal rights issue certainly has stoked up strong passions. In Britain, few other issues are capable of bringing so many people of apparent good will onto the streets; of causing otherwise quiet, politically inactive middle class citizens to pelt trucks (containing live animal exports) with rocks, form human barricades, break into laboratories to release captive animals into the wild, disrupt fashion shows and hunting meets, and bombard their politicians with letters of complaint about the abuse of animals.

True, Britain has been derided as a nation of "animal lovers," but such sentimentalism aside, one finds much hard-nosed, ideological resentment at the way animals are treated, resentment which can turn into action at a slight provocation. When the philosopher Michael Leahy published a book against animal rights [*Against Liberation*], he was subjected to a fierce hate campaign. Academics like Roger Scruton and Peter Carruthers have braved ridicule and even contempt for their philosophical opposition to animal rights. Most people, seeing the passion and commitment with which animal rightists defend their cause, think: "Surely people who can get so worked up about an issue have a point?" And when someone stands up to say that animals do not have rights, or that it is at least an arguable issue, in many eyes it is tantamount to saying: "It's OK to do what you like to animals—they've got no rights," where the special emphasis on the last few words is supposed to convey the idea that because they have no rights, they have no moral standing whatsoever.

It is time the animal rights issue, like the abortion and euthanasia issues, was looked at in a less emotionally charged and more philosophical way. It's time that some myths, often deliberately sown, were cleared up. Here are a few.

David S. Oderberg, "The Illusion of Animal Rights," *Human Life Review*, Spring/Summer 2000.
Copyright © 2000 by Human Life Foundation. Reproduced by permission.

Myth #1: If you think animals do not have rights, you must think it is all right to do anything to them, that their welfare does not matter. Myth #2: [Ardent animal rights activist] Peter Singer and his followers believe in animal rights. Myth #3: Traditional moralists, who are both pro-life and oppose animal rights but believe in animal welfare, can make common cause with what I will call revolutionary moralists, who are both pro-abortion and either believe in animal rights or take a Singerian consequentialist line giving no special moral priority to humans just because they are humans. . . .

So how do rights fit in? What is a right, anyway? In order to understand the concept of a right, we need to understand the concept of a good. Then we need to grasp why it is that paradigmatic holders of rights, namely human beings, have such a status; and we can then see why this status cannot be extended to other animals. To begin, a good can be defined as that end of an action which fulfills the nature of a thing. There are a number of goods which fulfill human nature, without which a human being cannot flourish or live a distinctively human life. These include such material things as food, shelter, warmth and health, but also things of a more psychological, emotional or intellectual nature, such as family, friendship, knowledge and understanding, work, play, artistic experience, and religion. These are some of the principal things which, to use Aristotle's term, fulfill us as rational animals. The absence of any of them diminishes our human dignity, our integrity—it leaves not just a quantitative but a qualitative gap in our lives.

But if human beings are rational animals, and have rights, this means some animals have rights—so why not others? What's so special about us humans? Isn't it arbitrary—to use Singer's term, "speciesist"—to say that human animals have rights but others do not. When we see how rights interact with goods, it becomes clear why it is not insofar as we are animals that humans have rights, but insofar as we are rational. A right is best thought of as a kind of protection conferred by morality. For example, my right to privacy means that I am protected by morality itself in my pursuit of the good which privacy constitutes, namely a sphere of activity which remains unknown to others. Without such a sphere of activity a person's integrity would be undermined; privacy is essential to human dignity, and is therefore a good. Now, like many goods it may not be protected by the legal system. But this does not mean we can invade each other's privacy, since morality itself confers protection: I have a moral right to privacy, and your violation of that right would be blameworthy unless justified by a greater right, say the right to life.

> ***"It is time the animal rights issue . . . was looked at in a less emotionally charged and more philosophical way."***

A right, then, protects a person in his pursuit of some good. It means that others are under a duty not to violate that right; that the right holder is morally permitted to exercise his right without hindrance; and even, in some cases, that he is permitted to use force in safeguarding his right (e.g. the right of self-defence). That is all well and good, say animal rights supporters—but why are animals excluded from being right holders? Don't they, just like humans, have whatever is necessary for the possession of rights? Why the distinction?

It is here that animal rightists start going off in different directions. Traditionalists need to ask them: "So what do you think is necessary and sufficient for the possession of rights, seeing as you are so sure animals possess them?" A number of proposals have been put forward. Perhaps the most sophisticated defence of animal rights has been set out by the philosopher Tom Regan, who groups a number of ideas together into a complex criterion which he calls being a "subject-of-a-life." Animals have rights, he says, because they are not mere "receptacles" of pain and pleasure, but conscious subjects with lives of their own just like us, goods to pursue just like us, and separate identities just like us. Now, I have no space to evaluate Regan's theory in depth. Instead I will briefly discuss the most important elements of his criterion, one or more of which are fixed on by animal rightists in support of their case.

> ***"A right is best thought of as a kind of protection conferred by morality."***

## Consciousness

The first is consciousness. Surely being conscious is enough for a creature to have rights? For a start, not all animals are conscious, so consciousness, if it conferred rights, would only confer them on some animals. But you might also ask: what is meant by consciousness? Here the animal rightists might mean several things, such as sentience (the capacity to feel pain and pleasure), perception, memory, a sense of the future, and various other features that make a creature a psychological subject. It is true that we humans have all of these things, but that doesn't mean that we have rights because we have these mental characteristics. The truth is that there is no straight entailment between consciousness in any or all of the respects just mentioned, and the possession of rights. What is the logical connection between sentience and rights? Feeling pain/pleasure is just another way that a creature's life can go badly/well for it, along with having or lacking food, having or lacking disease, and so on. So why don't plants have rights? They aren't sentient, but their lives can go well or badly in other ways. What is so special about pain and pleasure?

The same goes for perception, memory or a sense of the future. Why should we think that a creature has rights simply because it perceives or remembers or anticipates the future? Conceptually, none of these take us beyond sentience. The animal rightist might say that what matters is memory of self, and a sense of one's own future—but this brings in self-consciousness, which I will come to in a moment. For the present, it seems that sentience, perception, memory and a sense of the future guarantee that an animal is a psychological subject—but not that it is a moral subject. The animal rightist needs to bridge the conceptual gap between the two.

What about beliefs and desires, as well as other mental states such as being afraid, or contented, or sad—don't they guarantee that the animal possessing them has rights? To be sure, there is much philosophical debate about whether animals even have beliefs and desires, or other mental states such as those mentioned. (Note: it is the job of the philosopher to judge this, not the animal behaviourist—the issue is not just empirical but conceptual, though empirical evidence is of course relevant.) But I am prepared to accept for the sake of argument that some animals do have beliefs, desires and other mental states, even if their content is radically impoverished compared to human mental states. The question, however, is: Even if some animals have beliefs and desires, how does it follow that they have rights? Again, what is the logical connection between the two? It may be that an animal which has beliefs and desires (as well as perceptions, memories, and so on) has an inherent value in the sense that one can assess how well or badly its life is going independently of how useful it is to other creatures. But the same can be said for ants, amoebae and rose bushes. All that having complex mental states such as beliefs and desires does is to make the ways in which the possessor's life can go well or badly more subtle and complex: desires can be frustrated, beliefs can be the product of deception, memories can be disturbing, and so on. But none of this implies that animals which have these mental characteristics have rights.

***"There is no straight entailment between consciousness . . . and the possession of rights."***

Self-consciousness is one of the features which animal rightists most commonly refer to in support of their thesis. It is not mere awareness, they say, but awareness of self which confers rights; not a mere sense of the past or the future, but a sense of one's own past or future. Again, I am prepared to accept for the sake of argument that some animals are self-conscious, though there will not be many. Perhaps only higher apes such as chimpanzees are self-conscious: for one thing, they are capable of grooming themselves with a mirror and a comb. But whether the numbers are large or small, the familiar question reappears: what is the conceptual or logical connection between being self-conscious and having rights? How does being conscious of self add something importantly different from merely being conscious? What is important is not that an animal is self-conscious, but the way in which it is self-conscious, as I will explain. In fact, my argument against animal rights implies as a necessary consequence that right holders will be self-conscious, but self-consciousness is not part of what it means to possess rights.

A similar point can be made about another of the more common features appealed to by animal rightists: that some animals have language. The truth is that the empirical evidence for linguistic competence by animals is, despite the media propaganda, woefully inadequate. The only serious contenders are kinds of chimpanzee, but these creatures show very little if any ability to communicate using language. They can imitate, they can react, they can be conditioned—but the rest looks like the product either of wishful thinking, or of deliberate skewing of the evidence, by the scientists who hopefully observe them. But even supposing they did possess language—why should it follow that they had rights? There is a philosophical mistake involved in basing rights on language: language is a tool of communication, of interpersonal relation; and to ground rights in it would be to take a contractualist or communitarian view of rights, a view which held that a creature has rights because it is "in relation" to other creatures. Such a doctrine is both false and pernicious, as much when applied to the unborn child ("It can't communicate with others or enter into a meaningful relationship with others, therefore . . . ") as when applied to adult humans or any other creature. Having rights depends upon the way the creature itself is, not on what kinds of relationship it enters into. To be sure, it is a necessary consequence of having rights that a being has linguistic capacity as well as self-consciousness, but again having rights is not grounded in linguistic capacity.

Having put the main alternative views to one side, I can now say that what matters in the having of rights is twofold: (a) knowledge; (b) freedom. More precisely, a right holder must, first, know that he is pursuing a good, and secondly, he must be free to do so. No one can be under a duty to respect another's right if he cannot know what it is he is supposed to respect. Similarly, no one can call another to account over respecting his right if the former cannot know what it is the latter is supposed to respect. By "call to account" I mean making a conscious demand on them, even without speaking a word. How can the right holder make a conscious demand on another if he cannot know what he is demanding?

Again, no one is under a duty to respect another's rights if he is not free to respect or not to respect, if he is not able to choose between right and wrong. Similarly, no one can possess a right if he is not free to pursue the good it protects, if he is not capable of planning his life, ordering his priorities, choosing to live in a dignified and human way or a squalid and less-than-human way.

***"Having rights depends upon the way the creature itself is, not on what kinds of relationship it enters into."***

Now it becomes clear why animals—nonhuman ones—cannot possess rights. It is because they do not possess the two features which are necessary for being a right-holder. No animal knows why it lives the way it does; no animal is free to live in one way or another. Animals, from the smallest single-celled organism to the most human-like ape, are governed purely by instinct. That is why, for instance, even the most hard-line animal rightist does not advocate prison (or worse) for chimpanzees that go on random killing sprees, as they are known to do. Nor do they advocate forcible prevention of lions from eating gazelles—"They can't help it," it is said. And that is precisely the point: they can't. Such is the paradox at the heart of animal rightism.

## Animalistic Instincts

We humans are governed partly by instinct, of course: you do not get up every morning and think, "To eat or not to eat—that is the question"—you just go and make some toast! But note two things. First, the more animalistic our behaviour, the more instinctive it is. Food, drink, reproduction—these are the sorts of activities that are largely if not wholly instinctive. Secondly, no matter how instinctive, every such activity can come within the sphere of choice, or free will; otherwise there would be no hunger strikers and no celibates! As babies, when mentally handicapped or senile, or even comatose, humans may be governed far more by instinct than by knowledge and free choice, but this does not mean such people have no rights. They are still qualitatively different from other animals because of the kind of creatures they are; and so they have human rights just as much as the sleeping, the drunk and the drugged. Neither age, nor illness, nor abnormality can change the fundamental fact that all such people are instances of a distinctive kind of animal—free to choose and aware of why it does so.

> ***"Animals . . . are governed purely by instinct."***

Not so for the animal kingdom. No experiment that has ever been conducted into animal behaviour has demonstrated that animals know why they do what they do, or are free to choose one course of action over another. From insects to apes—all kinds of complex behaviour have been demonstrated, such as deception, tool-making, social group formation, mutual assistance. But nothing has been found which sets the ape apart from the insect in any qualitative sense bearing on freedom and knowledge of purpose. The "gee whiz" articles that appear in the popular press on a regular basis, revealing the latest trickery or intelligence on the part of some animal (usually an ape), are therefore useless as forming an empirical justification for regarding animals as metaphysically, in their nature, the same as human beings.

## Duties in Respect of Animals

Now to return to the myths I stated earlier. First is the supposition that if you think animals do not have rights, you also think it is OK to treat them however you like. But how does one follow from the other? Only if rights are the whole of morality, which I have said they are not. The traditional moral position is that although we have no duties toward animals, we do have duties in respect of them. We are not free to be cruel to them or cause them unnecessary suffering.

We are bound to look after and preserve the entire natural world that has been given to us, in a way consistent with our own flourishing as a species. Hence we are free to use animals for our benefit and for reasons that do not in themselves involve vice or immorality, such as food, modest clothing and scientific research that can benefit the life and health of man. But if this also means condemning fur coats as fashion accessories, or investigation into the latest ways of pandering to our human vanity (such as cosmetics research), so be it. I do not imagine the animal rights lobby will object. We are also free to hunt animals for the protection of our property, of the countryside, and even for leisure. None of this, however, licenses cruelty, bloodlust, or the deriving of pleasure from a sentient being's pain. The basic principle is one of modesty: the living of an unluxurious life, attention to necessities, and respect for God's creation.

***"Utilitarians do not believe in rights, for animals or humans."***

The second myth is that Singer and his followers believe in animal rights. As I have said in various places, and as cannot be repeated often enough, utilitarians do not believe in rights, for animals or humans. All that matters are the costs and benefits (however they are measured; some utilitarian comes up with a new way of calculating them every week). Singer himself is on record as saying: "I am not convinced that the notion of a moral right is a helpful or meaningful one. . . ." but that "[t]he language of rights is a convenient political shorthand. It is even more valuable in the era of thirty-second TV news clips. . . ." Now if that is not a case of the cynical manipulation of ethical debate for one's own advantage, I don't know what is. So for all that Peter Singer has performed the service of alerting us to the mistreatment of animals in farming, science and elsewhere, and pleading for a radical change in our attitude to animals, the animal rightists can forget it if they think they will find support in his writings for absolute opposition to meat-eating, absolute opposition to animal experimentation, or to any treatment of animals that would be inconsistent with their having basic rights.

The third myth is that traditionalist moral theorists can make common cause either with animal rightists or Singerian utilitarians. They cannot make common cause with the second group because Singer's defence of animals rests on a conceptual move the traditionalist can only abhor—the downgrading of human beings as just another animal, with no special rights (indeed no rights at all), no special status; with every human able, in the appropriate cost-benefit situation, to be sacrificed for the benefit of other humans, or even for the benefit of other animals. When it comes to animal experiments, for instance, Singer does not rule them out per se: all he pleads for is consistency. If we are prepared to use animals, he argues, we should be prepared to use brain-damaged babies (or maybe even normal babies) at a similar level of mental development (whatever that means). And since research on humans will tell us more about humans than research on other animals, science itself dictates that it is the baby who would be the most desirable experimental subject. The traditional ethicist, ought, I think, to be able to spot the Trojan horse that constitutes Singer's impassioned defence of animals. . . .

Perhaps, as implied earlier, we look in the wrong direction for the source of our modern brutality towards animals. It is not the traditional distinction between man and beast that needs correcting, but our own selves: the moral degeneracy which makes factory farming, bullfights and horrendous scientific experiments on animals a part of life. It is the lack of virtue, and flowering of excess, which has resulted in there being far more animal suffering in the world today than ever existed in prior ages.

# Only Humans Have Rights

**by Roger Scruton**

**About the author:** *Roger Scruton, a writer and philosopher living in England, is editor of the* Salisbury Review, *a quarterly journal of conservative thought.*

The U.S. Constitution specifies our rights but is silent about our obligations. The Founders took for granted that people knew what their duties were. After all, they were brought up on the Bible and the Ten Commandments, and it was no business of the state to remind them that they should live godly, sober, and righteous lives. The role of the state was to broker their disagreements, to make the space required for social peace, to ensure that no central power could oppress the individual citizen, and to prevent any body of citizens from ganging up against others or depriving them of their elementary freedoms.

## Using Rights to Cancel Duties

Admirable though this conception is, it assumes a condition of society that is no longer with us. The continuing emphasis on rights, in a world that has lost sight of its duties, is as much a fragmenting as a cohesive social force. This, surely, is the real meaning of the conservative complaint that an activist judiciary undermines the "moral majority." By constantly extending and amplifying the list of rights, the Supreme Court also depletes the reservoir of duties. Striking in this respect was the decision in *Roe v. Wade*, which deprived the unborn fetus of all rights under the Constitution, while discovering (conservatives would say, inventing) a "right of privacy" nowhere mentioned in the Constitution but strong enough nevertheless to override the primary duty of a mother toward her unborn child. What more vivid example could there be of the use of rights to cancel duties and at the same time to privilege the desires of present generations over the long-term interests of society? And what clearer example of the liberal attempt to "discover" constitutional rights whenever the cause requires them and regardless of what the Constitution says?

This is not to say that traditionalist views on abortion are right and the views of liberals wrong. It is simply to point to the far-reaching social effect of a legal

Roger Scruton, "Animal Rights," *City Journal*, vol. 10, Summer 2000. Copyright © 2000 by *City Journal*, www.city-journal.org. Reproduced by permission.

process that puts rights at the top of the agenda, and that encourages everyone, regardless of his social and moral standing, to sue for them. The long-term consequence will be to reduce majority values and life-styles to mere "options" among a range of socially valid alternatives, all of which will deserve equal respect from law and equal subsidy from the exchequer. This is already happening with homosexual "marriage"; it will extend, in time, to many other forms of relationship, in obedience to the urgent desire of this or that section of society to free itself from "outmoded" burdens or to enjoy some previously forbidden pleasure. Euthanasia is currently a crime. It will soon be a right—a right for which relatives can sue, and which they will use with a clear conscience to put their old parents out of their misery.

Still, there are limits. Rights may have taken precedence over duties, but American jurisprudence has always been clear that rights cannot be had for free. Every legal privilege creates a burden on the one who does not possess it: your right may be my duty, and people who claim rights are also in the business of respecting them. Rights cannot be invented without also inventing the social and legal relations that enable us to uphold them, and the shopping list of rights will therefore be severely limited by social custom and human nature. The conservative hope is that, at a certain point, common sense will prevail. "If you invent any more rights," people then will say, "you will find yourself in a society where nobody respects them. In other words, you will have destroyed the very benefit that you sought to extend." And it seems to me that the birth of "communitarianism" as a posture within the American liberal tradition is really a recognition of this possibility, and of the underlying truth that a society cannot be based in rights alone but must also inculcate a strong sense of duty in its members, if rights are to be anything more than useless bits of paper. Rights ought not to be given but purchased, and the price is duty. You can have many things on the cheap; but the moral life isn't one of them.

## Jeopardizing Human Dignity

But this brings us face-to-face with what is, to my mind, the strangest cultural shift within the liberal worldview, one that promises to sow even more confusion than liberalism inherently requires: the growing advocacy of "animal rights." Properly understood, the concept of a right—and the attendant ideas of duty, responsibility, law, and obedience—enshrines what is distinctive in the human condition. To spread the concept beyond our species is to jeopardize our dignity as moral beings, who live in judgment of one another and of themselves.

> ***"Rights cannot be had for free."***

In 1991, a group of animal-rights activists sued on behalf of Kama, a dolphin trained at great expense by the U.S. Navy and transferred to the Naval Ocean Systems Center in Hawaii from his previous home in a Boston aquarium. The suit held that Kama's life would be in jeopardy in his new environment, and that his rights were therefore violated by his forcible transfer. The court threw out the case on the grounds that Kama, being a dolphin, could not sue, either in Hawaii or in Massachusetts.

Now, a decade later, the lawyer who represented Kama, Steven M. Wise, has published a book, *Rattling the Cage*, which advocates the rights of animals and argues that a law granting rights to people but not to animals is no more tenable than a law granting rights to freemen but not to slaves. Jane Goodall, the gorilla ethologist, calls the book "the animals' Magna Carta," and Harvard has appointed its author to teach "animal-rights law"—by no means the first example of a professor appointed to teach a non-existent subject. Wise is also founder and president of Harvard's "Center for the Expansion of Fundamental Rights"—or "Center for Moral Inflation," as conservatives might prefer to call it.

Meanwhile, Princeton University's Center for the Study of Human Values has appointed the Australian philosopher Peter Singer, author of the seminal *Animal Liberation* (1975), to a prestigious chair, causing widespread disgust on account of Singer's vociferous support for euthanasia. (Defenders of animal rights not infrequently also advocate the killing of useless humans.) Singer's works, remarkably for a philosophy professor, contain little or no philosophical argument. They derive their radical moral conclusions from a vacuous utilitarianism that counts the pain and pleasure of all living things as equally significant and that ignores just about everything that has been said in our philosophical tradition about the real distinction between persons and animals. Although Steven Wise surprisingly makes no mention of Singer, their simultaneous prominence in the American academic establishment only further confirms the suspicion that animals are next on the agenda. . . .

***"Rights ought not to be given but purchased, and the price is duty."***

## Supreme Science

What are we to make of all this? Steven Wise's book contains a generous measure of legal and constitutional history, but no philosophy other than a few second-hand snippets. His authority is not philosophy but science—and in particular the studies in primatology that have told us how very like the apes we are, and how very like us are the apes. The movement in favor of animal rights is not merely the latest example of the "rights inflation" that liberals have always promoted. It is part of a larger movement of ideas away from the other-worldly dogmas of religion to the this-worldly theories of science. Science now stands at the apex of our beliefs, and a morality derived from any other source is apt to appear quaint and outmoded. And when science is in charge, duties sink still further into the background, since only God can give commands, and God is in retirement.

Of course, when science is used in this way, as the major premise in a revisionist morality, it is abused. Properly understood, science is silent about our duties; but it is also silent about our rights. It is not an alternative source of moral judgments, since it has no moral authority at all. The aim of science is to explain, not to justify. Good and evil, right and wrong, duty and freedom, are concepts that play no part in its theories and cannot be derived from them. Those who rely on science for their moral outlook depend heavily on popularizers like Stephen Jay Gould and Richard Dawkins, who make science seem relevant to our moral choices only by dressing its neutral theories in the borrowed clothes of judgment. No more influential book has appeared in recent decades than Dawkins's *The Selfish Gene*, the very title of which reveals how far the author is from true scientific thinking. To describe the gene as selfish is to think of it as a moral being, capable of generous and ungenerous actions. It is to re-assume the anthropomorphic and magical ways of thinking that science is supposed to dispel.

***"Science now stands at the apex of our beliefs."***

Still, given enough science to be struck by our resemblance to the apes, but not so much as to be reminded of the difference, you can easily fall into the new habits of mind exemplified by Wise and Singer. Instead of seeing man as the summit of creation, the vehicle of God's purpose on earth, and the sovereign over all other species, science tells us, according to Wise, that the human species is merely one branch of the great tree of evolution, with no privileged place in the scheme of things. And it is true that this is what modern science says.

## Humans Are Self-Created Beings

However, the scientific truth about *homo sapiens* is not the whole truth about mankind. We are members of the human species. But we are also persons and, as such, animated through and through by an ideal of what that species might achieve. The concept of the person has no place in biological science, for "person" is not a biological category. Nevertheless it is fundamental to all our legal and moral thinking. The Judeo-Christian tradition would explain the idea of the person in theological terms. But the concept is taken from Roman law (which in turn borrowed it from the theater: *persona* means mask), and it implies no theological commitment. A person is a potential member of a free community—a community in which members can lead lives of their own. Although other animals are individuals, with thoughts, desires, and characters that distinguish them, human beings are individuals in another and stronger sense, in that they are self-created beings. They realize themselves, through freely chosen projects and through an understanding of what they are and ought to be.

Negotiation, compromise, and agreement form the basis of all successful human communities. And this is the true ground of the moral distinction that we make, and ought to make, between our own and other species. The concepts of right, duty, justice, personality, responsibility, and so on have a sense for us largely because we deploy them in our negotiations and can invoke by their means the ground rules of social order. They define strategies with which we coordinate our social life, but which we can only use when dealing with others who also use them.

To use these strategies on animals is to misuse them; for if animals have rights, then they have duties too. Some of them—foxes, wolves, cats, and killer whales—would be inveterate murderers and should be permanently locked up. Almost all would be habitual law-breakers. All would deserve punishments from time to time, though maybe they could hire lawyers like Steven Wise to argue that they could not possibly be blamed, since only humans are blameworthy.

## Abusing Evolutionary Biology

As I suggested, science provides authority for this weird morality only when clothed in moral doctrine. The sleight of hand that gave us the "selfish" gene gives us the rights of baboons. By disguising anthropomorphic (in other words, pre-scientific) ways of thinking as science, Wise rediscovers the enchanted world of childhood, in which animals live as Beatrix Potter describes them, in an Eden where "every prospect pleases, and only man is vile." By abusing evolutionary biology in this way, we are able to read back the sophisticated conduct of people into the animal behavior that prefigures it.

But this means that the apes appeal to animal-rights activists for precisely the wrong reason—namely, that they look like people and behave like people, while making no moral demands. The apes are re-made as versions of ourselves, purged of the guilt that comes from the attempt to lead the life to which we, as moral beings, are condemned: the life of judgment. Nothing impedes our sympathy for the chimpanzee and the bonobo, since their lives are blameless. It is not that they do no wrong, but that "right" and "wrong" here make no sense.

And that explains, in part, the appeal of the animal-rights movement. It shifts the focus away from moral beings toward creatures in every respect less demanding—creatures like dogs, which return our affection regardless of our merits, or cats, which maintain an amiable pretense of affection while caring for no one at all (a fact always vehemently and fruitlessly denied by their keepers). The world of animals is a world without judgment, where embarrassment, remorse, guilt, and penitence are unknown, and where human beings can escape from the burden of moral emotions. In another way, therefore, those who tell us that we have no special place in the scheme of things create a place for us that is just as special. By focusing our human attitudes on animals, we are playing at God, standing always apart from and above our victims, smiling down on their inno-

> ***"Human beings are . . . self-created beings."***

cent ways, removed from the possibility of judgment ourselves, and, in our exaltation, imagining that we confer the greatest benefit on those whom we patronize.

## Rabbits as Pets

A case in point is the rabbit, an attractive animal, celebrated and humanized in children's literature. Alone in its cage, utterly dependent on the child who feeds it, bright-eyed and impassive as it is stroked and cuddled, the rabbit seems to be in its element: made for human companionship and basking in human love. It is the quintessence of the pet, mutely reflecting its owner's utterly fallacious view of himself as the kindly provider and justified guardian of this precious piece of life.

As a matter of fact, however, rabbits are gregarious animals, for whom there is only one mental torture greater than solitary confinement, which is that of being cuddled by a member of a large rabbit-eating species. The pet rabbit learns to adapt to its conditions, much as human beings learned to adapt to Stalin's gulag. Being unable to shift its eyes, the rabbit maintains its generous stare even when held by a smelly omnivore emitting vile drooling noises and smiling down on it with a mouth full of teeth. Correct behavior is rewarded, after all, with a piece of lettuce. In this way the rabbit teeters from terror to terror and from day to day.

> ***"It is not that [animals] do no wrong, but that 'right' and 'wrong' here make no sense."***

In the wild, however, in the teeming burrow where he mates promiscuously with his kind, where the only smell is the smell of rabbit, and where every intruder is regarded with abhorrence, the rabbit takes his revenge: eating crops, destroying saplings, and undermining paths and fields. Anybody who has had to contend with rabbits will know that these creatures, which by their nature are available in the wild only in large supplies, are far from lovable.

It is at this point that the advocate of animal rights steps in. Like the child, he imagines the rabbit still dressed in its Beatrix Potter trousers, enjoying a quiet domestic life below ground. For him the warren is just like a human community—founded by negotiation and agreement, structured by rights, and entitled to protection from the law. To shoot such defenseless animals seems to him like a crime, and he campaigns vigorously for a law that will make it so.

## Disrupting the Historical Equilibrium

Of course, he is selective in his passions: foxes, rabbits, and badgers can count on his support; rats and mice don't get a look in. But this only enhances the damage done to the historical equilibrium that has enabled humans and animals to live together on realistic terms. It is this equilibrium that is maintained by the old arts of hunting. And in those old arts you glimpse another, more ancient and more healthy relation between man and beast—the relation between Homer's Odysseus and the old hound Argus, first to recognize his master on his return to Ithaca, or the relation between Alexander and Bucephalus, which caused the conqueror to found a city in memory of his heroic horse. The unsentimental love between man and beast that comes about when they are engaged together in some act of war or predation is, indeed, the nearest that animals attain to equality with the human species—and it is a love that is deeply horrible to the defenders of animal rights for that very reason. For it is a love founded in the aspect of animals that they put out of mind—the relentless life-and-death struggle that is the normal condition of life in the wild.

***"'Working' relations with animals are not only good for the animals: they are also good for us."***

This love exists too, among the sworn enemies of rabbits—the keepers of ferrets, who solve the rabbit problem in nature's way. The ferret is as furry and appealing to the sight as a rabbit, and would feature in children's books, in some toothless version, were it not for the fact that nobody knows anything about it except those who know everything, and who love the ferret with the severe military love that attaches the falconer to his bird and the huntsman to his hounds. Our local ferreter lifts his precious animal from its box as though handling a newborn baby and coos to it quietly in a private language far richer in syllables than the sparse dialect that he keeps for human use. And when he slips the ferret into the warren and watches it slide into the darkness, his face is full of a tender anxiety, like the face of a father whose son is leaving for the wars.

Such "working" relations with animals are not only good for the animals: they are also good for us. For they are a strong reminder of the fact that, whatever we do, it is we who are in charge. Why is this? This question brings us full circle to the American Constitution and the vision on which it is founded—the vision of human beings as a distinct order of creation, the guardians of the natural order, answerable for their lives and duty bound to make the best of them. That is the vision that justifies our belief in rights as the necessary conditions of human fulfillment. Take away the moral life and its goal of human excellence, and the talk of rights becomes meaningless

The lover of baboons who goes to live with his tribe knows full well that he can regain civilization at any time; he goes armed with medicines and books and cameras—perhaps even with a mobile telephone. He respects and even loves the creatures with whom he lives, and is in his turn respected, after a fashion. But he knows that, when it comes to any real decision for the future, it is he alone who can make it. Indeed, there is no greater reminder of the distinctiveness of our condition than the emotions that overwhelm us in the presence of a tribe of apes. People like Jane Goodall, who take with them into the wild a spirit of creative compassion, exemplify Dante's words:

*Considerate la vostra semenza:*
*Fatti non foste a viver come bruti,*
*Ma per segue virtue e conoscenza.*

"You were not made to live as brutes but to follow virtue and knowledge."

If the apes survive, it will be because we decide (spurred on by Jane Goodall) to save their habitats. And the same will be true, in time, of virtually all the larger animals. And if domestic animals are bred and cared for, it is because we have an interest in their products. In all our dealings with the animals, the inherent mastership of the human race displays itself. And this only goes to show that we alone have the duty to look after the animals, because we alone have duties. The corollary is inescapable: we alone have rights.

# The Concept of Animal Rights Degrades Humans

**by David R. Carlin**

**About the author:** *David R. Carlin is a professor of philosophy and sociology at the Community College of Rhode Island, as well as the chairman of the Democratic Party in Newport, Rhode Island.*

[In 1999] Harvard Law School offered its first-ever course on animal rights. This is good news for animal rights advocates, since Harvard is one of the two or three top law schools in the nation. If Harvard is on board for animal rights, can the Supreme Court be far behind?

Currently, American law gives animals protection in a wide variety of circumstances, but it affords them no rights. The prevailing legal principle is that only persons can be bearers of rights. So, before animals can have rights, either that principle will have to be changed, or it will have to be shown that animals (at least some of them) are persons.

## Narrowing the Gap Between Humans and Animals

The animal rights movement (of which Peter Singer, the controversial Princeton professor, is the philosophical guru) contends that there should be only a relatively narrow legal gap between humans and animals. Biologically speaking, of course, there is only a narrow gap between humans and the highest of the animals. But this raises the question: Is a strictly biological account of human nature adequate? The animal rights movement would answer this question in the affirmative; Christianity, by contrast, has always answered it in the negative. At first glance, the animal rights movement seems to be aiming at the elevation of animals. In fact, however, it is but the latest episode in a long history of attempts to degrade humans.

Many individual members of the animal rights movement, I willingly concede, are kindhearted folks who are revolted at cruelty to animals and wish to minimize it; they have no desire to degrade humanity. But historical movements

David R. Carlin, "Rights, Animal and Human," *First Things: A Monthly Journal of Religion and Public Life*, August 2000, p.16. Copyright © 2000 by Institute on Religion and Public Life. Reproduced by permission.

often have objective tendencies that contradict the wishes of their proponents. (Witness communism, which, despite its objective tendency to tyranny and mass murder, had many followers who were humane and philanthropic in intention.) Underlying the push for narrowing the legal gap between humans and animals is the philosophical premise that there is no more than a narrow ontological gap between humans and animals. But the animal rights people are not the first to embrace this premise. Far from it.

In the sixteenth century, Michel de Montaigne, the great French essayist and skeptic, argued that the gap between humans and animals was narrower than most people imagined. He devoted much of his writing to showing that humans are not nearly as rational as we, in our pride, suppose ourselves to be, while occasionally pointing out how surprisingly rational the lower animals could sometimes be. In his most comprehensive and influential essay, "An Apology for Raimond Sebond," Montaigne cited the case of a logical dog, a case reported by an ancient philosopher. The dog was following a scent along a path. Suddenly the single path divided into three. The dog hesitated: Which way to go? He sniffed at one path; no scent. He sniffed at a second; no scent there either. And then, without bothering to give an investigatory sniff at the one remaining, he set off on this third path. Clearly the dog had performed a disjunctive syllogism, saying to himself. "The scent I'm following will be found either on path A, B, or C; it is not found on A or B; it follows, therefore, that it must be on C."

***"[The animal rights movement is] the latest episode in a long history of attempts to degrade humans."***

And since, according to the dominant philosophical tradition of Montaigne's day—a tradition that reached back to Plato, Aristotle, and the Stoics—rationality (or a capacity for logical thinking) is the distinctive characteristic of human beings, it was no small thing to show that dogs as well as humans can be logical. In the world of philosophy, it had always been rationality that established the almost infinite ontological gap between humans and animals. Show that rationality is a characteristic shared by both, and humanity's ancient claim to dominance is destroyed.

## Humans as Animals

Near the middle of the eighteenth century, during the robust early stages of the Enlightenment, a minor French philosophe, Julien Offroy de la Mettrie, wrote a book titled *L'Homme Machine*. If humans are nothing more than machines, he argued, albeit very refined and complex ones, then there is certainly no great ontological gap between humans and the lower animals, for they are also machines, though less refined and complex. La Mettrie suggested, for instance, that the reason apes cannot speak is not because of any inferiority in rationality to human beings but because of "some defect in the organs of speech."

He believed a young ape could be taught the use of language if we were to instruct it using the (then newly invented) methods used to teach deaf-mutes to "speak." In other words, given the right teacher, apes could be taught sign language.

But to date, the greatest of all attempts to narrow the gap between humans and the lower animals has been Darwinism. Perhaps this should not be said of the Darwinism of Darwin himself, who had little wish, at least in public, to extrapolate his biological findings into the realm of ontology. But it can certainly be said of many of Darwin's epigones, who viewed humans as purely biological entities and thus regarded biology as competent to pronounce the last word on the ontological rank of human nature. Since humans have the same remote ancestry as the rest of the animal kingdom, since we have the same relatively proximate ancestry as the great apes, and since anatomically we bear a strong resemblance to these our "cousins," then it follows (they reasoned) that humans are ontologically only a little bit superior to the lower animals. And if we measure superiority and inferiority in terms of capacity to survive (which is perhaps the true Darwinian way of measuring these things), then we are not superior at all; for it is obvious that all surviving animal species have equally met that test. By that measure, our superiority, if we are indeed superior, will not be shown until we outlast all other animal species; but that is almost certainly impossible, since it is difficult to imagine how humans could survive on earth without the assistance of other simultaneously existing animal species.

***"Show that rationality is a characteristic shared by [humans and animals], and humanity's ancient claim to dominance is destroyed."***

## Anti-Christian Motive

Our contemporary animal rights movement is heir to this long tradition of trying to narrow the gap between humans and lower animals. But what motive lies behind this tradition? The answer seems obvious enough. Specifically, the motive is anti-Christian; more generally, it is a strong animosity toward the view of human nature taken both by biblical religions and by the great classical schools of philosophy, especially Platonism and Stoicism. That man is "made in the image and likeness of God" is an expression found in the Bible, but it is a formula that well expresses the anthropology of Plato and the Stoics as well. To reduce human nature to nothing more than its biological status is to attack this ancient and exalted conception of human nature.

In defense of the attackers—from Montaigne, through the philosophes and the Darwinians, to Peter Singer (who once wrote a book titled *Animal Liberation*) and the Harvard Law School—it might be said that their intentions have often been humane. The Stoic-Christian theory of human nature, in their opinion, has been dangerously unrealistic, the product not of empirical observation but of fantastic imagination. By encouraging men and women to believe that their true home is not in this world, the world of nature—that we are potentially divine beings living in temporary exile—this fantastic theory has rendered humans unable to achieve such limited happiness as we might have achieved. Demoting human nature from heaven to earth will, by making us more realistic, render us more successful. Better to own an acre in Middlesex than a county in Utopia.

This defense ("they had good intentions") might have been acceptable prior to the twentieth century. But in the course of that century we had some unpleasant experiences with persons who entertained the purely biological conception of human nature. Hitler was a great believer in this purely biological conception (sometimes with a confused overlay of pagan romanticism). In his way, he can be counted as one of Darwin's epigones. Now, of course, you cannot prove that an idea is wrong simply because Hitler embraced it; for instance, that Hitler favored the production of Volkswagens doesn't prove that they are bad automobiles. But when there is a direct link between one of his major ideas and the Holocaust, as there is in the case of his conception of human nature, this is at least enough to give us pause. At present I cannot prove that the idea of animal rights is extraordinarily dangerous and inhumane; to get proof of this, we'll have to wait until the disastrous consequences of the idea reveal themselves over the next century or so. But I strongly suspect that it's a dangerous idea, and accordingly I suspect that the promoters of this idea, whatever their intentions, are enemies of the human race.

# Animals Are the Property of Humans

**by Richard A. Epstein**

**About the author:** *Richard A. Epstein is a professor of law at the University of Chicago Law School.*

The field of animal *law* is one of the oldest and most well-established branches of any legal system, wholly apart from the modern preoccupation with animal *rights.* It is therefore something of a trendy commentary on our times that the law courses offered at, for example, Harvard and Georgetown, are courses in animal rights, not animal law. These courses are taught, virtually uniformly it appears, solely by advocates on one side of the issue, most notably, perhaps, Steven M. Wise, the author of the much discussed recent book, *Rattling the Cage: Toward Legal Rights for Animals.* Briefly stated, Wise's position is that animals, especially chimpanzees and their close relations, the bonobo, are entitled to legal personhood, which at the very least guarantees them protection against exploitation and capture by man. His book is a passionate if one-sided treatment of a difficult and complex question, and it should surely strike an uneasy nerve in all of its readers, unless they are utterly devoid of the empathy that marks every well-developed human being.

## Disturbing Power

I can offer some personal evidence of the disturbing power of Wise's thesis. [In the summer of 1999] I took a phone call from William Glaberson of the *New York Times*, asking me to comment on the above-mentioned courses on animal rights. It was clear that most independent commentators were reluctant to speak on the record about this question. Perhaps I should have followed suit, but my contrarian nature led me to begin with the admission that I had not specialized in this particular topic, but had nonetheless over the years done a fair bit of scattered work about animals in connection with my other academic research. I have written on the rules that govern the liability for animals, on the rules for transfer-

Richard A. Epstein, "The Dangerous Claims of the Animal Rights Movement," *The Responsive Community*, Spring 2000, pp. 28–37. Copyright © 2000 by The Responsive Community—The Communitarian Network. Reproduced by permission.

ring ownership of animals, on the rules limiting the killing and capture on animals, and on the role of animals in medical research. It struck me then, as it continues to strike me now, that the problem of the proper treatment of animals is much more ubiquitous than is commonly supposed. The discussion therefore ranged in some detail on what I thought were the strengths and weaknesses of the animal rights movement. Then, as often happens in these close interviews, Glaberson published a *New York Times* story, "Legal Pioneers Seek to Raise Lowly Status of Animals," in which I was quoted in opposition to this latest legal juggernaut. "Would even bacteria have rights? There would be nothing left of human society if we treated animals not as property but as independent holders of rights."

***"Animal law generates its own fair share of debate."***

These pithy remarks generated a veritable deluge of phone calls and e-mail messages, and requests for interviews, radio, and TV shows. Not all the attention was, to say the least, complimentary. (For the record, I know that bacteria are not animals, and that irritability is not quite the same as sensation.) But in today's fast-paced world, two sentences on the front page of the *New York Times* was all it took to make me an expert on the question of animal rights, and for the next two weeks I was treated as a minor celebrity, besieged with requests to do radio and television shows on the subject. Since that time, further requests come in on a regular basis, including at least a half-dozen requests to comment on Steven Wise's book, and several to take on the unenviable task of debating him on the subject.

In this case, the press of popular concern has forced me to think harder about the subject than I have before, and has led me to see if I could work out to my own uneasy satisfaction a fuller account of the relationship between human beings and animals (yes, I am aware that human beings are themselves highly evolved animals) that might be advanced in opposition to views such as those that Wise presents. What follows is a sketch of some of those ideas.

## Animal Hybrids

The regulation and use of animals did not suddenly pop onto the social agenda. Rather, it has been with us from the beginning of human society. The early domestication of certain wild animals—horses, pigs, goats, cows and sheep (what Jared Diamond calls the major five in *Guns, Germs and Steel*)—was completed by 2,500 B.C. The success of that movement, as he demonstrates in great detail, was critical to the survival of all early cultures, as a source of food (meat and milk), agriculture (oxen pulling the plow), warfare (on horseback), fertilizer (no need to explain how), clothing (from leather and wool), and germ warfare (against unexposed populations).

In dealing with the legal status of animals, it is often said by writers like Wise that animals were treated as property, as mere things. But that assertion massively oversimplifies a difficult area of law, and is no more accurate than the common proposition that slaves were treated as things, when in fact from the earliest time they were governed by a set of rules that treated them as legal hybrids, part property and part human beings. It is not difficult to see how a rule of capture (he who takes an unowned thing from the state of nature may treat it as his own) applies in an easy fashion to a seashell or a stone. It is rather more difficult to apply that rule to animals who are able to elude capture, who may be wounded by one person and taken by another, or who may be able to escape to their original habitat after capture but before taming. Nor did the legal rules act as though animals were inanimate objects incapable of forming intentions. The rule was that an animal that left its owner's home with an intention to return (the so-called *animus revertendi*) could not be taken by another, while the animal that had regained its freedom in the wild could be so captured. The rules in question did not afford animals rights as such, although they did speak of how these animals could preserve or regain their natural liberty. Quite simply, the primitive people who were absolutely dependent on animals did not fall into any crude classification errors.

## The Importance Attached to Animals

What is clear is the importance they attached to animals. The harsh sanctions imposed on cattle thieves offer one unmistakable sign; the sacred forms of conveyances that ancient peoples used to transfer the ownership of an animal from one person to another offer yet another. The Romans, for example, reserved their most solemn form of conveyance (the *mancipatio*) to certain key draft animals, which they recognized as critical capital assets, matched or exceeded in value only by land. The law of tort discussed at great length the rules governing the liability for animals whose conduct caused harm to the person or the property (including the animals) of other persons.

> ***"None of our laws dealing with animals put the animal front and center as the* holder *of property rights."***

Elsewhere, we often poke fun at the notion of "noxal" liability (that is, the rule whereby an animal could be surrendered by its owner in lieu of payment of damages), or the rules governing animals *damage feasant* (whereby animals could be held as security for the damage caused to crops by straying cattle). But these rules facilitated the resolution of many low-level disputes between neighbors by sanctioning a self-help system that enjoyed widespread legitimacy in both ancient and modern farming communities. I could hold your animal until you paid for the damage it caused. Eventually, the legal system held owners directly liable for any serious injuries their animals caused to land, people, or other animals. Finally, the extensive trade in animals and animal products meant that animal resources could move in markets to their highest use, just like other resources, human and material.

During the 19th and 20th centuries, one weakness of this system of animal law became apparent. Its property-based rules provided no mechanism to prevent the systematic extinction of wild animals through overhunting and overfishing. To counter this risk, legal systems instituted, with varying degrees of success, rules that limited the catch of whales, fish, and wild game in order to counteract the "tragedy of the commons" that results when a hunter keeps his entire quarry but bears only a tiny fraction of the future loss of the stock. More recently, the more stringent protections afforded to endangered species have generated heated controversy, as farmers have claimed, rightly in my view, that they have been unfairly forced to stand aside while protected animals decimate their sheep and cattle herds, while receiving not a dime in compensation from the government. (Note that one question on which animal rights activists are eerily silent is the extent to which one kind of animal should be allowed by humans to kill and eat another.) Wholly apart from the new preoccupation of animal rights, animal law generates its own fair share of debate.

## The Separation of the Species

Behind these traditional debates lies one key assumption that today's vocal defenders of animal rights brand as "species-ist." Descriptively, they have a point. Sometimes the classical view treated animals as a distinctive form of property; at other times animals became the object of public regulation. In both settings, however, the legal rules were imposed largely for the benefit of human beings, either in their role as owners of animals or as part of that ubiquitous public-at-large that benefitted from their preservation. None of our laws dealing with animals put the animal front and center as the *holder* of property rights in themselves—rights good against the human beings who protect animals in some cases and slaughter them in others.

Our species-ist assumption is savagely attacked by the new generation of animal rights activists, whose clarion call for *person*hood—the choice of terms is telling—is a declaration of independence of animals from their human owners. Their theme generates tremendous resonance, but it is often defended on several misguided grounds.

***"The question . . . is not how many genes humans and chimpanzees have in common; it is how many traits they have in common."***

First, they claim that we now have a greater understanding of the complex behaviors and personalities of animals, especially those in the higher orders. Even though the fields of sociobiology and animal behavior have made enormous strides in recent years, the basic point is an old one. [Philosopher René] Descartes got it wrong when he said that animals moved about like the ghost in the machine. The older law understood that animals can be provoked or teased; that they are capable of committing deliberate or inadvertent acts. Sure, animals may not be able to talk, but they have extensive powers of anticipation and rationalization; they can form and break alliances; they can show anger, annoyance, and remorse; they can store food for later use; they respond to courtship and aggression; they can engage in acts of rape and acts of love; they respect and violate territories. Indeed, in many ways their repertoire of emotions is quite broad, rivaling that of human beings.

***"If pets are out, so too is the use of animals for medical science."***

But one difference stands out: through thick and thin, animals do not have the capacity of higher cognitive language and thought that characterizes human beings as a species, even if not shared at all times by all its individual members. We should never pretend that the case against recognizing animal rights is easier than it really is. But by the same token, we cannot accept the facile argument that our *new* understanding of animals leads to a new appreciation of their rights. The fundamentals have long been recognized by the lawyers and writers who fashioned the old legal order.

## Higher Primates

Second, animal activists such as Wise remind us of the huge overlap in DNA between human beings and chimpanzees. The fact itself is incontrovertible. Yet the implications we should draw from that fact are not. The observed behavioral differences between humans and chimpanzees are still what they have always been; they are neither increased nor decreased by the number of common genes. The evolutionary biologist should use this evidence to determine when the lines of chimps separated from that of human beings, but the genetic revelation does not establish that chimps and bonobos are able to engage in the abstract thought that would enable them to present on their own behalf the claims for personhood that Wise and others make on their behalf. The number of common genes humans have with other primates is also very high, as it is even with other animals that diverged from human beings long before the arrival of primates. The question to answer is not how many genes humans and chimpanzees have in common; it is how many traits they have in common. The large number of common genes helps explain empirically the rapid rate of evolution. It does not narrow the enormous gulf that a few genes are able to create.

Third, Wise and other defenders of personhood for animals have line-drawing problems of their own. If that higher status is offered to chimps and bonobos, then what about orangutans and gorillas? Or horses, dogs, and cows? All of these animals have a substantial level of cognitive capacity, and wide range of emotions, even if they do not have the same advanced cognitive skills of the chimps and bonobos. Does personhood extend this far, and if not, then why does it extend as far as Wise and others would take it? The frequent analogy of chimpanzees to slaves hardly carries the day, given the ability of individuals from different human populations to interbreed with each other and to perform the same set of speech and communicative acts. Nor is it particularly persuasive to note that individuals with serious neurological or physical impairments often have far less cognitive and emotional capacity than normal chimpanzees or dogs. For one, we in fact *do* recognize that different rules apply to individuals in extreme cases, allowing, for example, the withdrawal of feeding tubes from individuals in a permanent vegetative state. In addition, important human relations intrude into the deliberations. These human beings, whatever their impairments, are the fathers, mothers, sisters, and brothers of other human beings in ways that chimpanzees and bonobos are not.

Fourth, the animal rights activists often attack the question from the other side by offering bland assurances that people today do not need to rely on animal labor and products in order to survive as human beings. Typically, animal rights activists put their claims in universalistic terms. But in so doing they argue as though in primitive times animals and agriculture fell into separate compartments, when in truth they were part of a seamless enterprise. Animal power was necessary to clear the woods, to fertilize and plow the fields, and to harvest the crop. Meat and dairy products were an essential part of primitive diets. The early society that did not rely on animals for food, for labor, for warfare was the society that did not survive to yield the heightened moral sensibilities of today. It was the society that perished from its want of food, clothing, and shelter—a high price to pay for a questionable moral principle. And, if this new regime is implemented, the animal rights movement condemns millions of less fortunate people around the globe to death today. [In] March [2000] the *New York Times* ran a painful story about the question of whether the preservation of gorillas in Africa placed at risk the subsistence economies of the nearby tribes.

## Power Differentials

Today, perhaps people fortunate enough to live in prosperous lands could live without having to use animals for consumption or labor, but the long-term agenda, if not the immediate demands, of the animal rights activists cut far deeper. For activists such as Gary Francione of Rutgers-Newark Law School, the mere ownership of animals is a sin: no pets, no circuses, no milk, no cheese, no horses to ride, no dogs, cats, birds, or fish around the house. These relationships are condemned in good Marxist terms as being based on power differentials, and thus are barred: the animals who seem to like being pandered to suffer from, as it were, a form of false consciousness.

> ***"The arrival of human beings necessarily results in the death of some earlier animal occupants."***

Fifth, more ominously, if pets are out, so too is the use of animals for medical science. In dealing with this issue, Wise is brutally explicit in describing what it is for chimpanzees to suffer in isolation the final effects of the ravages of AIDS. No one could argue that this conduct did not cry out for justification. Yet by the same token, the question is could the conduct itself be justified? To answer that question in human terms, one has to look at the other side of the equation, and ask what has been learned from these experiments, what wonder drugs have been created, what scourges of human (and animal) kind have been eliminated. I do not pretend to be an expert on this subject, but so long as the vaccine for small pox comes from cows or the insulin for treating diabetes comes from pigs, then I am hard pressed to defend any categorical rule that bans all use of animals in medical experimentation. One has to have an accurate accounting of what is on the other side, and on that issue the silence of the animal rights activists is deafening.

***"No one can deny the enormous political waves created by animal rights activists."***

The argument here has its inescapable moral dimension. No matter what one's intellectual orientation, no one would—or should—dispute the proposition that animals should not be used in research if the same (or better) results could be achieved at the same (or lower) cost by test tubes and computer simulations alone. Nor would any one want future surgeons to try out new techniques on animals if they could be risklessly performed on human beings the first time out. But, alas, neither of these happy eventualities come close to being a partial truth. It is easy to identify many situations where human advancement comes only at the price of animal suffering. How to proceed then turns on the balance between these two unquantifiable considerations. For example, there exists today a dreadful shortage of human organs for transplantation and unless we are prepared to do animal studies on pigs and perhaps even chimpanzees, it is likely that we will postpone, perhaps forever, the day when genetically engineered animal organs could be successfully transplanted into human beings. If this be species-ism, then I plead guilty of the charge because I do rate the welfare of humans above that of animals, even as I, like many of those who work in veterinary medicine, care as well about the welfare of animals.

Sixth, medical research is not all that is at stake once the asserted parity between animal rights and human rights is acknowledged. Our entire system of property allows owners to transform the soil and to exclude others. Now if the first human being may exclude subsequent arrivals, what happens when animals are given similar rights? Their dens, burrows, nests, and hives long antedate human arrival. The principle of first possession should therefore block us from clearing the land for farms, homes, and factories unless we can find ways to make just compensation to each individual animal for its own losses. But I fail to see how this system would work, for to transfer animals from one habitat to another only unlawfully displaces animals at the second location. The blunt truth is that the arrival of human beings necessarily results in the death of some earlier animal occupants, even if it increases the welfare of others who learn to live in harmony with us. So if prior in time is higher in right, then we should fold up our tents right now and let the animals fight it out for territory, just as if we had never arrived on the face of the globe.

## The Current Legal Scene

The defenders of animal rights shrink, at least publicly, from the stark implications of their position, and dwell instead on their victories in court. But these claims are credible precisely because they have nothing whatsoever to do with their broader claims. Animal owners have recovered large awards for the malpractice of veterinarians. The damages paid are meant to cover not only the market value of the animal, but the loss of companionship to the owner. This is simply solid economics—for what the defenders of animal rights do not tell is that this outcome derives its power from recognizing that the actual losses *to the owner* exceed the market value of the animal, precisely because they include these nonmonetary elements. Similarly, it is commonplace today to allow one spouse to recover damages for loss of companionship from the injury or death of the other. But whether for humans or pets, the interests vindicated are those of the party who suffers the emotional and companionate loss, not that of the human or animal who has been injured or died. These cases therefore gain their resonance from a traditional property rights conception, from which the actions for consortium originally derived. It is hard then to see how they auger a new judicial age in which animals are set to have rights of their own against these same owners, vindicated by their human guardians. It is not as though the offspring of the deceased animal has an action for wrongful death.

A similar logic also applies to a 1998 decision in the District of Columbia, *Animal Legal Defense Fund, Inc. v. Glickman*. Here a zoo visitor was held to have "standing" to sue under the Animal Welfare Act of 1985, which provided generally that animals' keepers must meet conditions of confinement that ensure "the psychological well being of primates." That objective is certainly laudable in simple human terms, even if the new animal rights activists would shut down all zoos. But allowing a zoo visitor to sue to protect the zoo animals made it crystal clear that the rights vindicated by the action were those of the individual plaintiff, and not those of the animal. And no one doubts that Congress could reverse that decision by a statutory amendment that allows only for public inspection and enforcement of the provisions of the Act.

In sum, no one can deny the enormous political waves created by animal rights activists. (It is also easy to understand how their antiproperty theme gains many adherents from people who don't like private property for other reasons.) But it is another thing to endorse the agenda of the animal rights movement. Rules that prevent gratuitous cruelty to animals should be supported because animals suffer even if they do not think, at least as humans do. And we all know that animals are of enormous value to human beings, both in the wild and in captivity. It is, however, one thing to raise social conscience about the status of animals. It is quite another to raise the status of animals to asserted parity with human beings. That move, if systematically implemented, would pose a mortal threat to human society that few human beings would, or should, accept. We have quite enough difficulty in persuading or coercing human beings to respect the rights of their fellow humans to live in peace with each other. We have witnessed the Holocaust and other tragedies in our own time. And I must say that I find it offensive to think that anyone could find in the treatment of animals the same kind of senseless genocide, perverse evil, and unmitigated cruelty that marked those human tragedies. It is a massive intellectual and rhetorical mistake to press a concern with animals to that extreme. We should not undermine, as would surely be the case, the liberty and dignity of human beings by treating animals as their moral equals and legal peers. It would trivialize the slaughters of Hitler, Stalin, and Pol Pot by comparing them to the daily activity of slaughtering cattle. That is one kind of equivalence we must learn to fear. Animals are properly property. It is not, nor has it ever been, immoral for human beings, as a species, to prefer their own kind. What lion would deny it?

# Great Apes Do Not Have Legal Rights

**by David Wagner**

**About the author:** *David Wagner teaches constitutional law at Regent University in Virginia Beach and formerly was deputy counsel to the House International Relations subcommittee on International Operations and Human Rights.*

Why do we have rights, anyway? We should not take them for granted. The [twentieth century], after opening with such hopes for human advancement—or should I say, advancement through [the courts]—has witnessed some of history's most systematic and horrific denials of rights. The Nazis denied that Jews were rights-bearing beings; the Communists treated their real and perceived political opponents the same way. In the last ten years, the Serbs and Croats have done the same to each other.

All these examples involve denials of rights. So the solution might seem obvious: Never deny any rights claim. But, even if this advice is wise, it is not the advice we heed as a society. For instance, the Supreme Court tells us that unborn human beings are not rights-bearing beings, and Princeton University has just given a chair in ethics to a professor who teaches that rights are, in effect, lost whenever the death of the (former) rights-bearer would cause a greater increase in the total quantum of happiness than would her continued living. As a society, we accept some rights claims, we reject others—and the choices can be agonizing.

## Enter the Animal Rights Movement

Into this moral maelstrom comes the animal-rights movement, urging us to extend recognition as rights-bearing beings to animals, beginning with those animals whose mental functioning are judged to be most like our own—the great apes. To say the least, this effort will force us to think harder than ever before about how we decide when to recognize rights and what the origins of rights are.

Our nation's historical experience with the issue of race has made us rightly

David Wagner, "Symposium: Q: Should Great Apes Have Some of the Legal Rights of Persons?" *Insight on the News*, November 1, 1999. Copyright © 1999 by News World Communications, Inc. Reproduced by permission.

suspicious of any assertion that begins, "They don't have rights because. . . ." No matter how you finish that sentence, you're going to risk committing grave injustices and (what is even more frightening for some people) aligning yourself on the wrong side of history. We want to be very sure we're right before we assign a cutoff point to rights.

> ***"The problem with basing rights on intelligence . . . is that it leads to morally unacceptable conclusions with regard to mentally handicapped human beings."***

At the same time, we have so far rightly declined to adopt a burden-shifting scheme in which all demands for the expansion of rights presumptively are to be granted unless their opponents prove beyond a reasonable doubt that the moral framework of millennia is justified by an appropriate abstract theory. Such a shift in the burden of proof would lead to a necessary sequence of revolutionary rights claims: If great apes, why not all primates? If all primates, why not all mammals? All animals? All living things, including plants? And now that we're there, just what is the basis of our legal tradition's arbitrary discrimination between the living and the nonliving? What is its theoretical justification? If it has none—or none that qualifies as compelling—then bring on rocks' rights, etc.

## Claims of Intelligence

The best argument available to advocates of animal rights is the one that bases rights claims on intelligence. This argument holds that the human/non-human distinction was never more than a placeholder for the real distinction we ought to be making—the real distinction our forebears meant to make and would have made if they had been as clever as we are—which is the distinction between the more intelligent and the less intelligent. This distinction makes intuitive sense, which is why the animal-rights movement leads with the cause of the great apes, leaving the felines, rodents and invertebrates for tomorrow's debate.

The problem with basing rights on intelligence, though, is that it leads to morally unacceptable conclusions with regard to mentally handicapped human beings. Mildly retarded human beings are among the most loving and generous, and even the severely retarded can enrich the lives of others by providing grateful outlets for others' self-giving. Yet, if we adopt a rigid intelligence standard to valid rights claims, mentally challenged human beings would be ripe for the slaughterhouse or, rather, the involuntary euthanasia center. This conclusion would not follow, of course, if we were using a combined standard whereby rights are recognized in human beings and in intelligent nonhumans. The human retarded then would be protected by their status as humans, if not by their IQs.

But for some animal-rights advocates, humanness is to be dropped altogether as a standard for the possession of rights. Professor Stephen M. Wise, for instance, writes in a 1988 *Vermont Law Review* that "being human is neither necessary nor sufficient for dignity rights and that at least those nonhuman animals who possess a full or realistic capacity for autonomy should be eligible for dignity rights as liberty rights." This implies, however, no protection for humans whose capacity for autonomy is not "full or realistic." Their humanness, by itself, will not save them.

In order to avoid the danger of committing injustice by improvidently finishing the sentence, "They don't have rights because . . . ," it would seem urgent that any expansion of rights into the animal realm be cumulative, not alternative. If we add animals to the protected realm, we must not expel any humans. Any animal-rights doctrine that fails to include this safeguard may open itself up to a suspicion of harboring an antihuman agenda.

## Potential for Intelligence

It may be possible to avoid the overly restrictive implications of an intelligence-based standard by focusing instead on potential for intelligence, rather than actual or present intelligence. Thus, great apes would be deemed to possess rights because they belong to a species whose members normally have the potential for intelligence, and a human being with a severe mental handicap would be deemed to possess rights for the same reason. Notice, however, that we are now back to species-specific standards and have, to that extent, abandoned intelligence as a standard. In other words, we are making categorical decisions based on species membership—the very thing alleged to be an injustice at the start of this debate.

Another issue raised by focusing on potential rather than actual intelligence is that we would be required to attribute rights to unborn human beings. This would present a clearer case than even the mentally handicapped human being because the latter, barring a miracle, will never have ordinary intelligence, but the human unborn generally will.

Still another possibility is to focus on mere sentience. This certainly would bring in almost all mentally handicapped human beings; it also would bring in most animals, and the human unborn from an early point in pregnancy.

> ***"The capacity of human beings to give and demand reasons for their actions was the basis of their rights and duties."***

Attribution of humanlike status to nonhuman animals (I might as well have used the politically incorrect term subhuman since it is interchangeable with nonhuman in this context) would come at a cost that cannot be measured simply in terms of impediments to medical research, stricter standards for zoos, abolition of meat-eating or the like. Even to argue about rights for animals is to engage in the practice of exchanging arguments and developing reasons to justify actions. This is a uniquely human capacity. Perhaps we cannot say with certainty that moral action is uniquely human: Dolphins and great apes may choose one course of action over another because it's the right thing to do; even dogs can be taught to look shamefaced when the master says, "Bad dog." Moral action may not be uniquely human but sustained moral reflection about action is. Over millennia, we have moved from tribal, particularist concepts of rights to more universal and inclusive ones.

## Human Uniqueness

But this expansion has a logical end point: Humans are nonarbitrarily different. There is a remarkable consensus of both religion and philosophy on this uniqueness. The Stoic philosophers identified the key factor as speech. Judaism was the first to proclaim that God made man in His image and that He revealed Himself to mankind. Later on, Christianity proclaimed a radical redemption for all humankind, rooted in the claim that God Himself had taken on human nature. Later still, the Renaissance and the Age of Science taught their own version of human uniqueness, summed up by Shakespeare's Hamlet when he said: "What a piece of work is man, how noble in reason, how infinite in faculties, in form and moving how express and admirable; in action how like a god: the beauty of the world, the paragon of animals."

***"The animal-rights movement may have some valuable lessons for us."***

Continuing this tradition, [Immanuel] Kant, teacher of ethics to a world that no longer reflexively respected religious authority, taught that the capacity of human beings to give and demand reasons for their actions was the basis of their rights and duties. And, finally, our Founding Fathers declared that the American experiment was based on certain self-evident truths, beginning with the truth that all men are created equal, that they are endowed by their Creator with certain unalienable rights. Notice the constant copackaging of certain ideas: human uniqueness, capacity for reason-giving and special divine creation.

The anthropology of Genesis 1:27—"And God created man in His own image, in the image of God He created him: male and female He created them" (New American Standard Bible)—stretches throughout the great tradition of religion and philosophy. The scriptural account tells us, of course, that God created the other animals as well, but He created humans with a special type of consciousness, first mentioned in Genesis 4:26: "Then men began to call upon the name of the Lord." In the words of the Second Vatican Council: "The dignity of man rests above all on the fact that he is called to communion with God."

To reground rights on some lab-testable feature of humanity (such as intelligence) rather than on humanity itself would implicitly deny this great consensus. It would deny mankind's unique consciousness and unique relationship with the rest of nature. We would have to adopt a far more material—indeed, materialist—view of ourselves. This was not the view of mankind that led to the creation of literature, music, philosophy, science and industry. The greatest of great apes cannot write a story; he cannot even respond to one the way most human children can. Human achievement presupposes the anthropology of Genesis 1:27.

The animal-rights movement may have some valuable lessons for us when it comes to humane reforms of animal experimentation or proper maintenance of zoos. But we should decline its invitation to view ourselves as different only in degree, and not in kind, from the animals.

Chapter 2

# Is Animal Experimentation Justified?

# Animal Experimentation: An Overview

**by Harold D. Guither**

**About the author:** *Harold D. Guither is emeritus professor of agricultural policy at the University of Illinois at Urbana-Champaign. He has taught courses in the economic history of agriculture and agricultural food policy issues, and conducted research on other public policy matters.*

Probably the most intense controversy generated by animal rights activists involves the value and benefits of biomedical research. Ten federal government agencies conduct or sponsor laboratory tests with animals including the Departments of Agriculture, Defense, Energy, Interior, and Transportation. The US Department of Agriculture estimated that 106,191 dogs and 33,991 cats were used in registered research facilities in fiscal year 1993.

[Animal Rights activist] Andrew Rowan reports that for the six species, dogs, cats, primates, rabbits, hamsters, and guinea pigs, the 1990–1993 average use was 1,228,419. Since 1968, the use of these six species for research has declined about 50 percent. However, rats and mice account for about 80 to 90 percent of the laboratory animal total. The best research community estimates show about two-thirds of the dogs and all of the cats used in research and education are from pounds or shelters rather than bred for research.

According to [Professor] Bernard Rollin, animals used in research are identified in six categories although these groups oversimplify very complex activities:

1. Basic biological research with little concern for the practical application.
2. Applied basic biomedical research—the formulation and testing of hypotheses about diseases, dysfunction, genetic defects, new therapies, and treatments.
3. The development of drugs and therapeutic chemicals and biologicals.
4. The testing of various consumer goods for safety, toxicity, irritation, and degree of toxicity. Such testing may include testing of cosmetics, food additives, herbicides, pesticides, and industrial chemicals.

Harold D. Guither, *Animal Rights: History and Scope of a Radical Social Movement*. Carbondale: Southern Illinois University Press, 1998. Copyright © 1998 by the Board of Trustees, Southern Illinois University. All rights reserved. Reproduced by permission.

5. The use of animals in educational institutions and elsewhere for demonstration, dissection, surgery practice, induction of disease for demonstration purposes, and high school science projects.

6. The use of animals for extraction of products—serum from horses, musk from civet cats, and other products. This is not strictly research.

Rollin emphasizes that it is important to understand the type of research or testing that may involve animals. Animal activists and organizations may take different positions on these different categories.

## The Issues

The issues surrounding animal research focus on these questions:

1. How much regulation should government place on scientists engaged in research with animals?

2. Should proposed research projects be screened for possible benefits before they are undertaken?

3. With the large number of animal research projects and investigators, is the responsible government agency enforcing all applicable rules, regulations, and laws associated with animal research?

4. How should protection of animals from pain and suffering be balanced with the scientific process and hoped-for benefits to humans?

5. Should animals used in research be obtained from licensed dealers and animal shelters or bred and raised specifically for research purposes?

6. Could fewer animals be used in some experiments and obtain reasonably accurate results?

7. Can alternative methods be used to replace the use of animals in research, in testing of drugs and household products, in professional medical or veterinary education, and in other classroom and laboratory teaching?

## The Arguments Against Using Animals in Research

The first opposition to use of animals in research dates back to the late nineteenth century with the beginnings of the antivivisection societies. However, the opposition in recent years has emerged as animal activists and antivivisectionists object to causing animals pain and suffering in experiments that they believe have questionable benefit. Biomedical research scientists must now justify what they are doing and the expected benefits from animal research since animal activist opponents, basing their beliefs more on philosophical than scientific reasoning, have attempted to influence public opinion against their work. . . .

Animal activists, antivivisectionists, and some scientists are now less willing to accept reassuring statements from scientists that all is well in animal research activities. The opposition to animal research is based on concerns of whether

- some assumptions about animal testing are valid;
- laboratory science can make further contributions;

- basic research in the medical sciences has any direct bearing on preventing diseases or improving medical care;
- improvement in health is likely to come in the future, as in the past, from modification of the conditions that lead to disease, rather than from intervention in the mechanism of disease after it has occurred;
- billions of dollars are being wasted regulating substances that might pose little risk;
- animal research is a perpetuation of cruel and archaic methodology;
- the government should guarantee that animals are treated humanely;
- peer review by scientists assumes that only worthwhile and critically important projects are funded;
- animal research is the best way to discover cures and treatments for human diseases;
- money spent on animal experimentation should be made available for preventive measures that could save a far greater number of human lives;
- research results are relevant only to the species under tests and concern for the risk of misleading predictions, since humans and animals often respond quite differently to drugs and disease;
- the choice of species is based on nonscientific considerations such as cost, ease of handling, and laboratory tradition rather than anticipated similarity to people;
- human disease can be studied through animals; in the past, efforts to investigate cholera failed to induce anything similar in animals while contemporary scientists are having the same difficulty with AIDS; and
- animals have certain rights not to be used in ways that would bring pain or suffering.

> ***"Animal activists and antivivisectionists object to causing animals pain and suffering in experiments that they believe have questionable benefit."***

Research opponents recognize that the knowledge and the health benefits that have arisen out of bioscientific animal abuse cannot be denied or unlearned. But they also argue that spiritually evolving human beings no longer need to proceed in this direction and our inherent fear of death cannot be eliminated but can be spiritually modified.

Those who believe in scientific antivivisectionism feel they have the basis for directly challenging the medical establishment. The real point as they see it is that progress in medicine is not synonymous with improvement in human health. They believe that more lives can be saved through preventive measures than interventive technology. Although these lives may be different lives, they are just as important. . . .

The supporters for using animals in research believe that such research provides many benefits to humans based on scientific evidence. The value of medical research is recognized for extending the scope and precision of hygienic measures, immunization, and therapy and for providing an understanding of the body and its diseases. Strong support for using animals in research comes from those who have the most experience in doing that research and those who have seen the major benefits.

**"The knowledge and the health benefits that have arisen out of bioscientific animal abuse cannot be denied or unlearned."**

Dr. Michael E. DeBakey, chairman of the Foundation for Biomedical Research, emphasizes, "Not one advancement in the care of patients—advancements that you use and take for granted every day—has been realized without the use of animal research." Major professional groups approving the use [of] animals in research include the National Academy of Sciences Institute of Medicine, the National Association for Biomedical Research, the American Medical Association, and the American Veterinary Medical Association.

The National Academy of Sciences Institute of Medicine (NAS) presents a very personal perspective on animal research benefits: "Animal experiments have provided valuable information on the effects of visual stimulation on brain development, biofeedback techniques, memory loss, programmed instruction in education, aggression, stress, and recovery after strokes or brain injury. We would know much less about these aspects of human life without animal research, and continued animal research is essential if new ways are to be found to cope with behavioral problems."

Of the Nobel prizes awarded in medicine or physiology in the twentieth century, 54 of 76 were based on animal research. Among these have been the prize awarded for the studies using dogs that documented the relationship between cholesterol and heart disease, the studies using chickens that linked viruses and cancer, and the studies using cattle, mice, and chicken embryos that established that a body can be taught to accept tissue from different donors if it is inoculated with different types of tissue prior to birth or during the first year of life, a finding expected to help simplify and advance organ transplants in the future. Studies using animals also resulted in the successful culture of the poliomyelitis virus, the discovery of insulin, and the treatment of diabetes. . . .

## Alternatives to Animal Research

Finding alternatives for animals in research is not a simple process. The Johns Hopkins Center for Alternatives to Animal Testing has received generous grants and gifts to sponsor research dealing with alternatives. Andrew Rowan of Tufts University concludes, "Scientific interest in the topic of alternatives has been marked by legislative initiatives and campaigns by animal advocates against animal testing. However, the topic is also marked by rhetoric that has served to confuse the public and others."

Within the animal rights movement, the debate over research tends to focus on three exclusive methods: (1) regulating the use of animals through legislation; (2) abolishing the use of animals altogether; and (3) searching for alternatives to the use of animals.

Alternatives research is a relatively new approach and may not give immediate or spectacular results. In the short run, the search for replacements may eliminate fewer animals than regulation would. But over a longer period of time, the replacement approach should eliminate many more animals in research. Supporters of alternatives suggest a step-by-step process in which the need for animals is first reduced and then possibly eliminated in many scientific areas. But to replace animals in various tests, valid alternatives to the use of animals must be found.

The Food and Drug Administration (FDA) points out that many procedures intended to replace animal tests are still in various stages of development. Ultimately, testing must progress to a whole, intact living system, an animal. Not using animal tests when necessary would subject humans and other animals to unreasonable risks.

## No Substitute

In many areas of biologic and medical research, the NABR [National Association for Biomedical Research] insists that there are no substitutes for the study of living animals. "Many of the processes that occur within the human body remain too complex to be simulated by a computer or cell culture. We face too many terrible health problems—like cancer, AIDS, heart disease, Alzheimer's disease, birth defects and mental illness—to eliminate the animal research that has been responsible for so many advances in medical care."

> ***"[Many] believe that more lives can be saved through preventive measures than interventive technology."***

David Weibers, speaking before members of HSUS [Humane Society of the United States], emphasized, "We should not be under any false illusions that all of the findings of animal research can be reproduced in a computer model or tissue culture given our current level of technology and understanding."

Carl Cohen also dismissed as a serious error the thought that alternative techniques could soon be used in most research now using live-animal subjects. He emphasizes that no other methods now on the horizon, or perhaps ever to be available, can fully replace the testing of a drug, a procedure, or a vaccine, in live organisms.

AFAAR [American Fund for Alternatives to Animal Research] attempts to foster interest among scientists through grants to fund research in alternatives. However, validating alternatives to animals in research takes time, personnel, and money. Most researchers generally hold that nonanimal experiments are adjuncts rather than alternatives to animal experiments. Studies that do not use animals can produce much valuable information, but they cannot completely replace the information gained from animal experiments, they believe. . . .

The public basically agrees with the argument that animal research is necessary. But many are not entirely comfortable with the feeling that their health depends on practices that often cause death and possible distress of animals. The Scientists Committee for Animal Welfare stresses that if an effective debate on animal research and alternatives is to develop, then the question is not whether animals should be used at all but how both animal distress and the number of animals used in the laboratory might be reduced.

## Three R's for Animal Research

British scientists have argued that animal researchers should follow the principle of the "three R's"—replacement, reduction, and refinement. *Replacement* refers to situations in which nonanimal techniques may be substituted for techniques using research animals. For example, rabbits are no longer used in pregnancy tests. Using mice to test the potency of yellow fever vaccine was long ago replaced by a cell culture test.

*Reduction* refers to cases where the number of animals required for a particular activity or project can be reduced. Most toxicologists now agree that it is not necessary to use from sixty to two hundred rodents to generate a statistically precise lethal dose when perfectly adequate lethal dose data can be obtained using ten to twenty animals. The National Cancer Institute now uses cell culture screening systems and has reduced animal use by 80 to 90 percent, a decision based on scientific rather than animal welfare reasons.

*Refinement* refers to the modification of a technique to reduce the pain and distress experienced by research animals. For example, various jacket and tether systems have been developed to protect catheters inserted into research animals that allow an investigator to administer doses of test chemicals and take blood samples from an animal without having to restrain it.

## Promoting Humane Laboratory Animal Care

[Animal Rights activist Peter] Singer points out that most people may be unaware that scientists can be animal welfare advocates. The public may also be unaware of the difficulties of the research process. Furthermore, Singer asserts that the scientific community recognizes its professional obligation to safeguard and improve the welfare of laboratory animals. The National Institutes of Health published the first federal laboratory animal guidelines in 1955. In 1966, the US Department of Agriculture developed the first federal regulations under the *Animal Welfare Act.* Congress amended the *Animal Welfare Act* as part of the *Food Security Act of 1985.* Since then, standards for animals in research facilities have been established to ensure that pain and stress to the animals are minimized. Each research facility is required to permit inspection and to report annually that the rules are being followed.

However, implementation of the law may be limited by the staff to carry out inspections and enforcement. The US Office of Technology assessment report showed that on one list of 112 testing facilities, 39 percent were not even registered with the branch of the Department of Agriculture that inspects laboratories. Rats, mice, and birds are still excluded. Although a lawsuit attempted to include these animals, an appeals court overruled the lower court order.

The National Agricultural Library, officially a unit of USDA [United States Department of Agriculture], was also required to establish an information service on employee training and animal experimentation to reduce animal pain and stress. To provide public accountability and assure humane care of laboratory animals, training and recognition programs have been established.

Formed in 1965, the American Association for Accreditation of Laboratory Animal Care (AAALAC) represents national professional scientific, medical, and educational organizations and promotes high standards for animal care, use, and well-being through the accreditation process. Any laboratory animal program that uses and cares for animals in research, teaching, or testing can qualify for the voluntary accreditation program. Members of the accreditation council visit laboratory sites to inspect the facilities and consult with the staff. The AAALAC has developed guidelines for proper laboratory animal care that are accepted by the biomedical community and complement AAALAC accreditation programs as well as government regulations.

***"Many are not entirely comfortable with the feeling that their health depends on practices that often cause death and possible distress of animals."***

The American Association for Laboratory Animal Science (AALAS) is a professional, nonprofit organization of persons and institutions concerned about the production, care, and study of laboratory animals. The organization provides a medium for the exchange of scientific information on all phases of laboratory animals' care and use through its educational activities and certification programs. It has been certifying laboratory animal technicians for more than twenty years. The certification program has been accepted as a professional endorsement of an individual's general level of technical competence in animal care.

## The Debate over Human and Animal Values

Research on humans is considered immoral since it causes pain and infringes on their freedom. If certain kinds of research on humans is considered to be immoral, then philosophers argue that such research is immoral when conducted on animals.

Much of the debate over animals in research centers on the values of how people view animals, humans, and their relationships. The animal-oriented philosophers argue that there is no clear-cut line between humans and animals from a moral point of view and that animals have moral rights from their nature, even as humans do.

A fundamental distinction exists between the reformists who believe that animal research should continue, with various modifications or restrictions, and the abolitionists who believe that it should simply stop because, they believe, certain classes of animals have a moral status and should not be exploited. Others have expressed support for basic research but question certain types of animal testing.

***"Much of the debate over animals in research centers on the values of how people view animals, humans, and their relationships."***

In calculating the consequences of animal research, many scientists would ask the public to weigh the long-term benefits of the results achieved—to animals and to humans—and in that calculation, not have people assume the moral equality of all animal species. In a sense, this is a utilitarian philosophy, in some ways similar to Peter Singer's philosophy, which suggests that all lives are not equal.

## Freedom from Needless Pain

AVMA [American Veterinary Medical Association] points out that most research can be conducted with minimal pain to the animals and that scientists accord animals the right to freedom from needless pain but not the right to self-determination. The rights of animals will expand as technology and understanding reduce reliance on them, the AVMA asserts. But most scientists do not believe they should apologize for the higher value they place on humans.

In addition, the AVMA believes that animals play a central and essential role in research, testing, and education for continued improvement in the health and welfare of human beings and animals. The association also recognizes that humane care of animals used in research, testing, and education is an integral part of those activities. AVMA maintains that use of animals is a privilege carrying with it unique professional, scientific, and moral obligations. It encourages proper stewardship of animals but defends and promotes the use of animals in meaningful research, testing, and education programs.

AVMA also endorses use of "random-source" animals, if carefully controlled, since the association believes this practice contributes greatly to improving the health and welfare of both animals and human beings. Random-source animals are those obtained from pounds and shelters, cost less, and can be used for practice surgery in veterinary colleges or for other uses that do not require uniform size, genetics, or known health background. However, AVMA encourages adequate funding for investigation and enforcement activities to prevent cruelty and enhance the welfare of animals. . . .

Animal research has become more costly and difficult, in part because of self-regulation by scientists but also because of externally imposed regulation. Some animal researchers have left the field, and young researchers have chosen not to enter it. The biomedical research community would like to see every possible measure taken to limit the number of animals used and to find new testing methods. However, most researchers strongly believe that replacement of animals entirely is impossible at present. Scientists most actively involved in the search for and development of nonanimal techniques concur that animal testing must continue. The unthinkable alternative is to risk human safety and human lives.

# Animal Experimentation Is Justified

**by Stuart Derbyshire**

**About the author:** *Stuart Derbyshire is an assistant professor at the University of Pittsburgh Medical Center and a contributor to* Animal Experimentation: Good or Bad?

• Animal research has played a major part in the development of medicine, and will continue to do so.

• Yet scientists are becoming increasingly apologetic about their work.

• Regulations brought in to protect animals' welfare are hindering vital research.

• There is no 'middle ground' between animal research and a broader concern with animal welfare.

• Scientists who research with animals have made a moral choice—to put human life first. They should mount a robust defence of their work.

Animal research has been an integral part of the development of modern medicine, has saved an incalculable number of lives, and prevents tremendous human suffering. Yet it continues to be an issue of major political controversy. . . .

But where are the scientists in this debate? A strong case for more animal research could easily be made. Yet scientists appear increasingly apologetic about their actions.

I would argue that scientists have made a series of disastrous tactical errors in dealing with the animal rights movement, and they continue to do so. Most of the errors have to do with trying to accommodate to the animal rights movement, or to reason with it and make compromises.

## Scientists on the Defensive

The most widespread accommodation is the adoption of 'the three Rs', first proposed in 1959 following a report for the Universities Federation for Animal Welfare (UFAW). The three Rs are 'refinement', 'reduction' and 'replacement'.

Stuart Derbyshire, "Animal Research: A Scientist's Defense," *Spiked*, March 29, 2001. Copyright © 2001 by Spiked, Ltd. Reproduced by permission.

Scientists pledge to refine their techniques so as to induce the minimum amount of suffering; reduce the number of animals used; and replace animals with other techniques wherever possible.

At first blush the three Rs appear reasonable, if somewhat patronising. All animal experimenters know to reduce the amount of stress an animal is subjected to (refinement) so as to not hinder discovery—a stressed animal will be less likely to behave or respond normally. Equally, all researchers will naturally tend to use fewer or less-costly animals or techniques (reduction and replacement) so as to get quicker results for fewer resources.

Patronising or not, the three Rs were not developed from the perspective of good scientific practice. They were developed from the perspective of animal welfare. This makes the three Rs disastrous, reinforcing a lowlife opinion of animal researchers and encouraging the notion that animal experiments are problematic.

Once the 'perspective' of the animal is adopted it is inevitable that all experimentation will be seen negatively, as no animal experiments are in the interests of the animal. Adoption of the three Rs comes across as a confession of guilt. The impression is that research animals are a 'necessary evil', when in fact they are necessary, period.

## Losing Nerve

The defensiveness of scientists indicates that we have lost the collective nerve to make our case. Scientists have retreated from the public platform, preferring to keep their laboratory doors closed and their research techniques a secret. Experiments are performed under conditions of security matched only at military institutions.

When scientists are occasionally forced into the spotlight of debate, they speak in euphemism to hide the unpleasant details of their work. One example is the way medical researchers talk about animals' deaths. Animals may be 'sacrificed' or 'euthanised', but never 'killed'. This strategy is painfully shortsighted because it insulates the public from the realities of science, and hands animal activists an easy propaganda weapon. The activists show the reality—gruesome pictures and films of animals in their death throes—and in the process highlight that biomedical science is covering up, hiding a gruesome scene, implying shame of their own activities.

> ***"No animal experiments are in the interests of the animal."***

The concessions to animal rights, made by the adoption of the three Rs and the shroud of secrecy covering animal research, belittle the history of the medical breakthroughs made possible by such research. Worse, these concessions limit the potential for further research and ultimately make the principle of continuing animal research impossible to uphold.

## A History of Success

In 1908, Viennese researchers Karl Landsteiner and Erwin Popper conducted an experiment on monkeys. They removed part of the spinal cord of a boy who had died of polio. They ground it up, filtered it and injected it directly into the spines of two monkeys. One became paralysed. Both died. The spinal cords showed the same damage as those of humans with polio.

In a brilliantly simple way, Landsteiner and Popper had demonstrated that monkeys could be used to model human diseases. Other scientists quickly caught on. In 1911, monkeys were found to be susceptible to measles. In 1914, mumps. In 1928, yellow fever.

Landsteiner wanted to take his development and run with it, but getting the animals was expensive, inefficient and slow. His superiors encouraged him to abandon his monkey research and to use rats instead. Landsteiner ignored them and continued working on the few rhesus macaque monkeys that he could get.

## Discovering the Rh Factor

Landsteiner had won the Nobel Prize for his discoveries of blood types in humans in 1930, and he pursued the same types of questions in the macaque. In 1940 he discovered a blood factor shared by the macaques and humans: the so-called 'Rh' factor, short for rhesus.

***"Primate research helped . . . improve chemotherapy."***

Rh factor refers to a cluster of highly reactive proteins on the surface of red blood cells. Most people have these proteins and are called Rh positive. A minority, however, lacks the proteins and is called Rh negative. If an Rh-negative woman becomes pregnant with an Rh-positive child, her immune system will develop an immune defence that will attack any future pregnancy with an Rh-positive child. Her immune system will rip into the fetus' alien red blood cells, jamming them together and exploding them.

Before the discovery of Rh factor several thousand children were born brain damaged or dead due to Rh incompatibility. The majority of children in state mental hospitals were the result of Rh complications. Landsteiner's discovery led to the development of a vaccine that blocked the viscous immune response.

The following decades brought more abundant fruit from the animal research tree. In the 1950s, primate researchers developed chlorpromazine, one of the most powerful drugs used to treat mental illnesses such as schizophrenia. In the 1960s, monkeys were used to develop a vaccine against rubella, and in the surgical transplanting of corneas to restore vision. In the 1970s and 80s, primate research helped track down tumor viruses, to improve chemotherapy.

The now widely used vaccine for hepatitis B was developed largely in chimpanzees. The current vaccine candidates against AIDS were all developed using primates.

Researchers learned to do organ transplants using macaque monkeys. Potent anti-rejection drugs, such as Cyclosporin, were first used in non-human primates. The design of the heart-lung transplant was developed in rhesus macaques. The physiological connection is close enough that surgeons have attempted heart and liver transplants from baboon to human.

> ***"Without animal research, many . . . areas of work will grind to a halt."***

Californian surgeon Leonard Bailey put the heart of a baboon into an infant girl in 1989; Pittsburgh surgeon Thomas Starzl has twice attempted to transplant baboon livers into human patients with collapsing liver function. These early experiments failed but they pave the way for the future of xenotransplantation, and both surgeons have stated that they will try again.

## Nonprimate Animals

Primates are generally the most useful animals, because of their close kinship with humans; but other animals have also been put to good use. Control of diptheria came from guinea pigs and horses. Open-heart surgery was developed in dogs as was the technique of kidney transplantation. The critical diabetes work, leading to the development of insulin, was also done in dogs. From sheep came control of anthrax, and from cows the eradication of smallpox.

The surprisingly close fit between the human and mouse genomes means that there are many mouse models developed and in development to study genetic diseases, including cystic fibrosis and muscular dystrophy. The best hope for the reversal of paralysis currently involves severing the spinal nerves of rats and successfully growing the nerves back.

Ongoing research with a wide variety of animals includes investigations of AIDS, cancer, heart disease, development of artificial arteries, ageing, spinal cord injury, leprosy, malaria, Parkinson's disease, Alzheimer's disease, epilepsy, obesity, nutrition, infertility, *in vitro* fertilisation and a variety of birth defects.

Without animal research, many of these areas of work will grind to a halt, and all will suffer setbacks causing human tragedy. It was recently the 20-year anniversary of the first kidney transplant, and its pioneer, Thomas Starzl, was asked why he used dogs in his work. He explained that his first series of kidney transplant operations left the majority of his subjects dead. He figured out what enabled the minority to survive and commenced a second series of operations; the majority of these subjects lived. A third group of subjects received liver transplants and only one or two died. In his fourth group all subjects survived.

Starzl remarked that it is important to realise that his first three groups of subjects were dogs, while the fourth group was human babies. Was he supposed to experiment and refine his technique on humans, or was he expected to abandon a promising line of research that has saved innumerable lives? It is remarkable that we even have to consider the question.

It is unfortunate that there are not more scientists of Starzl's integrity. Too many are losing their perspective. Dr Keith Reimann, for example, does AIDS-related research in monkeys at Harvard University's animal facility. He insists that a macaque be killed as soon as it becomes sick, even if additional information might be gained by following the course of the illness. Such action is immoral, and it may also be self-defeating.

The many thousands of patients with end-stage AIDS are unlikely to be grateful for Dr Reimann's 'humane' action, and if it later becomes important to study end-stage AIDS, a whole new colony of monkeys will need to be infected to do the work that Dr Reimann might already have completed. Dr Reimann should take a leaf from Donald Silver's outlook. He did cancer studies on mice at Sloan-Kettering Hospital in the 1970s, and whenever he had doubts about the work, he had only to think about the terminally ill patients in the children's ward.

It is a necessary fact that animals will die and suffer in the pursuit of human betterment. By all estimates, at least one million monkeys died in the race to halt polio. By the early 1960s, when vaccine production was running smoothly, a previously dreaded disease that crippled or killed 20,000 people a year in the USA alone was afflicting a few people per year.

Cases of polio became so unusual that an occurrence anywhere was startling. It is a sobering thought that such an effort would, in all likelihood, be impossible today.

## Barriers to Research

The success of the anti-vivisection movement, and the difficulty of performing animal research, is apparent to any researcher proposing an animal experiment.

In the UK [United Kingdom], following the 1986 Animals (Scientific Procedures) Act, the researcher has to obtain a licence from the Home Office, and the proposed research must be part of a programme of work authorised by a project licence. The process of licencing involves an assessment of the invasiveness of the study and the species used, following the principles of the three Rs.

Invariably, considerable justifications for any procedures that involve distressing the animal will be required, and considerable pressure for the use of fewer animals, from further down the phylogenetic tree (such as using rats rather than primates), will be applied.

***"Animals will die and suffer in the pursuit of human betterment."***

The regulatory process is less stringent in the USA, but still restrictive. In 1985 Congress passed the improved Standards for Laboratory Animals Act, which provides laboratory-animal-care standards enforceable by US Department of Agriculture (USDA) inspectors.

Currently the Act does not cover rats, mice, birds, horses and farm animals, placing more than 95 percent of US animal research beyond the reach of the USDA. Consequently, there is no specific law requiring ethical assessment of nearly all proposed animal experiments, although in practice one is almost always required.

Virtually all universities have their own Institutional Animal Care and Use Committees (IACUCs), which voluntarily assess any proposed research with respect to the three Rs and provide assurance to grant awarding bodies that the research is animal welfare-friendly. Nevertheless, the process is voluntary and each institution has some discretion to organise its animal work as it needs to rather than according to government diktat as in the UK.

## Future Uncertainty

Unfortunately it is unclear how long the USA will hold off from legislation to cover rats, mice and birds. In 1990 humane organisations sued to have these animals included, on the basis of their own 'harm' at seeing animals mistreated. The plaintiff held the USDA responsible and initially won. In one of the most remarkably sensible judgments, the appeals court threw the case out on the basis that only those injured—in this case, the rats, mice and birds—can bring civil suit. Yet the USDA has since promised to include these animals within the next five years.

Moreover, a future case might succeed, meaning that an activist 'plant' in a laboratory need only claim distress at the way the animals are being treated to bring a nuisance lawsuit against the laboratory. Even without victory as precedent, a current accusation of wrongdoing, no matter how ludicrous and trumped-up, will lead to weeks or months of work stoppage while the laboratory is investigated by government agencies.

***"The barriers to research . . . are more than unfortunate."***

The barriers to research, whether governmental or institutional, are more than unfortunate. This tightening regulation of research stifles creativity and threatens human wellbeing. The more that regulations demand specific end points and justifications for using animals, rather than focusing on the clarity of the hypotheses and the strength of the researcher and his designs, the less creative the research will be and the more the possibility of discovery will be diminished.

It is unlikely that researchers today will follow the example of those like Landsteiner, who were able to chase their hunches and instincts in the pursuit of discovery.

## The 'Middle Ground': Seeking the Impossible

Unlike their contemporaries of a hundred years ago, US scientists seem only minimally interested in preventing legislation to proscribe their conduct. Scientists in the UK appear to be willing it on.

Organisations that have responded against animal rights propaganda, including Seriously Ill for Medical Research (SIMR), the Research Defence Society

(RDS) and the American Foundation for Biomedical Research, rightly trumpet the advances of medical research. This implies opposing regulation restricting animal research, and supporting the advancement of animal experiments wherever and however they are liable to be of benefit to humanity.

> ***"US scientists seem only minimally interested in preventing legislation to proscribe their conduct."***

SIMR, RDS and similar organisations, however, show a reticence towards promotion and have, paradoxically, supported much of the current legislation limiting animal research. Rather than trying to win the argument for why it is right to use animals in research, they have tried to meet the protesters half way, by addressing their concerns regarding animal welfare and by committing themselves to the three Rs and a gradual reduction of animal experiments.

The process of attempting to find a middle ground has gone the furthest in the UK, where the argument over animal research is most violent and vocal. In 1992 Colin Blakemore, professor of physiology at the University of Oxford, and anti-vivisectionist Les Ward, director of Advocates for Animals, began a correspondence and a series of exploratory meetings that culminated in the formation of the Boyd Group. The group includes anti-vivisectionists, animal welfare advocates, veterinarians, philosophers, scientists using animals, and funding bodies.

The group's objectives are to promote dialogue and, where there is consensus, to recommend practical steps towards achieving common goals. It has published four reports, and has encouraged the Home Office to require an ethical review process in every research establishment. It has also welcomed the decision by the UK government not to issue any further licences for the use of animals in testing cosmetics.

## Problematic Philosophy

Beyond the fact that the Boyd Group is adding to the legislative burden impeding any potential animal researcher to begin work, the entire philosophy of forming such a group is problematic. It is evident that the Boyd Group will never be able to propose an increase in animal research, because the anti-vivisectionists will oppose it and break the condition of consensus. On the other hand, it is likely that scientists will be able to propose alternatives to animal research, and these proposals will gain consensus.

The net effect of all this will be to add to the ratcheting down of animal experimentation, and to the palpable public suspicion that animal experiments are cruel and unnecessary.

The supposed 'middle ground' shared by researchers and animal rights activists is illusory. The reality is that greater accommodations will be provided to the animal rights activists at the cost of future animal experimentation and discovery. The agendas are diametrically opposed, and any compromise, including concessions to animal welfare, will only lead towards the ultimate abolition of vivisection.

It makes no sense for animal researchers to engage in a discussion of animal welfare beyond ensuring that the animals will be properly housed, fed and exercised, and that they will be generally physically and behaviorally nourished as much as possible to benefit their performance as an experimental subject. The idea that we should—or even can—be any more concerned about their welfare stretches credibility.

***"The supposed 'middle ground' shared by researchers and animal rights activists is illusory."***

Giving animals AIDS and other diseases, carrying out experimental surgeries and infusing untested drugs hardly sound like procedures aimed at protecting the animals' welfare. Mistreating animals is unacceptable because it ruins experiments—but any further concern for the animals' wellbeing is beside the point.

## One Way or the Other

Animal researchers and their advocates cannot have it both ways. Professed concern for the welfare of laboratory animals is simply inconsistent with the reality of laboratory experiments that almost invariably result in distress and death for the animal. The fact is that medical research is not concerned with the welfare of animals, and nor should it be.

The aim of medical research is to get answers about diseases and problems that afflict humanity. Taking a course that retards that progress is an affront to humanity in general and a particularly acute blow to those individuals whose very lives depend on that progress. Defending the welfare of animals means placing the life of a mouse, rat, cat, dog, monkey or whatever above that of the seriously ill.

Those of us who research with animals, or support the benefits of such work, have made a moral choice. We place human wellbeing and health above that of animals and we unequivocally believe that human life comes first. We must be willing to come out of our high-security research bunkers, stop hiding behind euphemisms and niceties, forgo attempts to make peace with our detractors, and stand by our decision.

# Animal Research Is Vital to Medicine

## by Jack H. Botting and Adrian R. Morrison

**About the author:** *Jack H. Botting, a retired university lecturer, is the former scientific adviser at the Research Defense Society in London. Adrian R. Morrison is director of the Laboratory for Study of the Brain in Sheep at the University of Pennsylvania School of Veterinary Medicine.*

Experiments using animals have played a crucial role in the development of modern medical treatments, and they will continue to be necessary as researchers seek to alleviate existing ailments and respond to the emergence of new disease. As any medical scientist will readily state, research with animals is but one of several complementary approaches. Some questions, however, can be answered only by animal research. We intend to show exactly where we regard animal research to have been essential in the past and to point to where we think it will be vital in the future. To detail all the progress that relied on animal experimentation would require many times the amount of space allotted to us. Indeed, we cannot think of an area of medical research that does not owe many of its most important advances to animal experiments.

### Louis Pasteur

In the mid-19th century, most debilitating diseases resulted from bacterial or viral infections, but at the time, most physicians considered these ailments to be caused by internal derangements of the body. The proof that such diseases did in fact derive from external microorganisms originated with work done by the French chemist Louis Pasteur and his contemporaries, who studied infectious diseases in domestic animals. Because of his knowledge of how contaminants caused wine and beer to spoil, Pasteur became convinced that microorganisms were also responsible for diseases such as chicken cholera and anthrax.

To test his hypothesis, Pasteur examined the contents of the guts of chickens suffering from cholera; he isolated a possible causative microbe and then grew

Jack H. Botting and Adrian R. Morrison, "Animal Research Is Vital to Medicine," *Scientific American*, February 1, 1997. Copyright © 1997 by Scientific American, Inc. Reproduced by permission.

the organism in culture. Samples of the culture given to healthy chickens and rabbits produced cholera, thus proving that Pasteur had correctly identified the offending organism. By chance, he noticed that after a time, cultures of the microorganisms lost their ability to infect. But birds given the ineffective cultures became resistant to fresh batches that were otherwise lethal to untreated birds. Physicians had previously observed that among people who survived a severe attack of certain diseases, recurrence of the disease was rare; Pasteur had found a means of producing this resistance without risk of disease. This experience suggested to him that with the administration of a weakened culture of the disease-causing bacteria, doctors might be able to induce in their patients immunity to infectious diseases.

***"The investigation of [infectious diseases] indisputably relied heavily on animal experimentation."***

In similar studies on rabbits and guinea pigs, Pasteur isolated the microbe that causes anthrax and then developed a vaccine against the deadly disease. With the information from animal experiments—obviously of an extent that could never have been carried out on humans—he proved not only that infectious diseases could be produced by microorganisms but also that immunization could protect against these diseases.

Pasteur's findings had a widespread effect. For example, they influenced the views of the prominent British surgeon Joseph Lister, who pioneered the use of carbolic acid to sterilize surgical instruments, sutures and wound dressings, thereby preventing infection of wounds. In 1875 Queen Victoria asked Lister to address the Royal Commission inquiry into vivisection—as the queen put it, "to make some statement in condemnation of these horrible practices." As a Quaker, Lister had spoken publicly against many cruelties of Victorian society, but despite the request of his sovereign, he was unable to condemn vivisection. His testimony to the Royal Commission stated that animal experiments had been essential to his own work on asepsis and that to restrict research with animals would prevent discoveries that would benefit humankind.

## Vaccines and Antibiotics

Following the work of Pasteur and others, scientists have established causes of and vaccines for dozens of infectious diseases, including diphtheria, tetanus, rabies, whooping cough, tuberculosis, poliomyelitis, measles, mumps and rubella. The investigation of these ailments indisputably relied heavily on animal experimentation: in most cases, researchers identified candidate microorganisms and then administered the microbes to animals to see if they contracted the illness in question.

Similar work continues to this day. Just recently, scientists developed a vaccine against *Hemophilus influenzae* type B (Hib), a major cause of meningitis, which before 1993 resulted in death or severe brain damage in more than 800 children each year in the U.S. Early versions of a vaccine produced only poor, short-lived immunity. But a new vaccine, prepared and tested in rabbits and mice, proved to be powerfully immunogenic and is now in routine use. Within two months of the vaccine's introduction in the U.S. and the U.K., Hib infections fell by 70 percent.

Animal research not only produced new vaccines for the treatment of infectious disease, it also led to the development of antibacterial and antibiotic drugs. In 1935, despite aseptic precautions, trivial wounds could lead to serious infections that resulted in amputation or death. At the same time, in both Europe and the U.S., death from puerperal sepsis (a disease that mothers can contract after childbirth, usually as a result of infection by hemolytic streptococci) occurred in 200 of every 100,000 births. In addition, 60 of every 100,000 men aged 45 to 64 died from lobar pneumonia. When sulfonamide drugs became available, these figures fell dramatically: by 1960 only five out of every 100,000 mothers contracted puerperal sepsis, and only six of every 100,000 middle-aged men succumbed to lobar pneumonia. A range of other infections could also be treated with these drugs.

The story behind the introduction of sulfonamide drugs is instructive. The team investigating these compounds—Gerhard Domagk's group at Bayer Laboratories in Wuppertal-Elberfeld, Germany—insisted that all candidate compounds be screened in infected mice (using the so-called mouse protection test) rather than against bacteria grown on agar plates. Domagk's perspicacity was fortunate: the compound Prontosil, for instance, proved to be extremely potent in mice, but it had no effect on bacteria in vitro—the active antibacterial substance, sulfanilamide, was formed from Prontosil within the body. Scientists synthesized other, even more powerful sulfonamide drugs and used them successfully against many infections. For his work on antibacterial drugs, Domagk won the Nobel Prize in 1939.

***"It is hard to envisage how new and better vaccines . . . can be developed without experiments involving animals."***

A lack of proper animal experimentation unfortunately delayed for a decade the use of the remarkable antibiotic penicillin: Alexander Fleming, working in 1929, did not use mice to examine the efficacy of his cultures containing crude penicillin (although he did show the cultures had no toxic effects on mice and rabbits). In 1940, however, Howard W. Florey, Ernst B. Chain and others at the University of Oxford finally showed penicillin to be dramatically effective as an antibiotic via the mouse protection test.

Despite the success of vaccines and antibacterial therapy, infectious disease remains the greatest threat to human life worldwide. There is no effective vaccine against malaria or AIDS: physicians increasingly face strains of bacteria resistant to current antibacterial drugs; new infectious diseases continue to emerge. It is hard to envisage how new and better vaccines and medicines against infectious disease can be developed without experiments involving animals.

## Other Areas of Medicine

Research on animals has been vital to numerous other areas in medicine. Open-heart surgery—which saves the lives of an estimated 440,000 people every year in the U.S. alone—is now routine, thanks to 20 years of animal research by scientists such as John Gibbon of Jefferson Medical College in Philadelphia. Replacement heart valves also emerged from years of animal experimentation.

The development of treatments for kidney failure has relied on step-by-step improvement of techniques through animal experiments. Today kidney dialysis and even kidney transplants can save the lives of patients suffering from renal failure as a result of a variety of ailments, including poisoning, severe hemorrhage, hypertension or diabetes. Roughly 200,000 people require dialysis every year in the U.S.; some 11,000 receive a new kidney. Notably, a drug essential for dialysis—heparin—must be extracted from animal tissues and tested for safety on anesthetized animals.

Transplantation of a kidney or any major organ presents a host of complications; animal research has been instrumental in generating solutions to these problems. Experiments on cats helped develop techniques for suturing blood vessels from the host to the donor organ so that the vessels would be strong enough to withstand arterial pressure. Investigators working with rabbits, rodents, dogs and monkeys have also determined ways to suppress the immune system to avoid rejection of the donor organ.

The list continues. Before the introduction of insulin, patients with diabetes typically died from the disease. For more than 50 years, the lifesaving hormone had to be extracted from the pancreas of cattle or pigs; these batches of insulin also had to be tested for safety and efficacy on rabbits or mice.

When we started our scientific careers, the diagnosis of malignant hypertension carried with it a prognosis of death within a year, often preceded by devastating headaches and blindness. Research on anesthetized cats in the 1950s heralded an array of progressively improved antihypertensive medicines, so that today treatment of hypertension is effective and relatively benign. Similarly, gastric ulcers often necessitated surgery with a marked risk of morbidity afterward. Now antiulcer drugs, developed from tests in rats and dogs, can control the condition and may effect a cure if administered with antibiotics to eliminate *Helicobacter pylori* infection.

> ***"There are no basic differences between the physiology of laboratory animals and humans."***

## Answering the Critics

Much is made in animal-rights propaganda of alleged differences between species in their physiology or responses to drugs that supposedly render animal experiments redundant or misleading. These claims can usually be refuted by proper examination of the literature. For instance, opponents of animal research frequently cite the drug thalidomide as an example of a medicine that was thoroughly tested on animals and showed its teratogenic effect only in humans. But this is not so. Scientists never tested thalidomide in pregnant animals until after fetal deformities were observed in humans. Once they ran these tests, researchers recognized that the drug did in fact cause fetal abnormalities in rabbits, mice, rats, hamsters and several species of monkey. Similarly, some people have claimed that penicillin would not have been used in patients had it first been administered to guinea pigs, because it is inordinately toxic to this species. Guinea pigs, however, respond to penicillin in exactly the same way as do the many patients who contract antibiotic-induced colitis when placed on long-term penicillin therapy. In both guinea pigs and humans, the cause of the colitis is infection with the bacterium *Clostridium difficile.*

> ***"No outstanding progress in the treatment of disease occurred until biomedical science was placed on a sound, empirical basis through experiments on animals."***

In truth, there are no basic differences between the physiology of laboratory animals and humans. Both control their internal biochemistry by releasing endocrine hormones that are all essentially the same; both humans and laboratory animals send out similar chemical transmitters from nerve cells in the central and peripheral nervous systems, and both react in the same way to infection or tissue injury.

Animal models of disease are unjustly criticized by assertions that they are not identical to the conditions studied in humans. But they are not designed to be so; instead such models provide a means to study a particular procedure. Thus, cystic fibrosis in mice may not exactly mimic the human condition (which varies considerably among patients anyway), but it does provide a way to establish the optimal method of administering gene therapy to cure the disease. Opponents of animal experiments also allege that most illness can be avoided by a change of lifestyle; for example, adoption of a vegan diet that avoids all animal products. Whereas we support the promulgation of healthy practices, we do not consider that our examples could be prevented by such measures.

Our opponents in this debate claim that even if animal experiments have played a part in the development of medical advances, this does not mean that they were essential. Had such techniques been outlawed, the argument goes, researchers would have been forced to be more creative and thus would have invented superior technologies. Others have suggested that there would not be a gaping black hole in place of animal research but instead more careful and respected clinical and cellular research.

In fact, there was a gaping black hole. No outstanding progress in the treatment of disease occurred until biomedical science was placed on a sound, empirical basis through experiments on animals. Early researchers, such as Pasteur and the 17th-century scientist William Harvey, who studied blood circulation in animals, were not drawn to animal experiments as an easy option. Indeed, they drew on all the techniques available at the time to answer their questions: sometimes dissection of a cadaver, sometimes observations of a patient, sometimes examination of bacteria in culture. At other times, though, they considered experimentation on animals to be necessary.

We would like to suggest an interesting exercise for those who hold the view that animal experiments, because of their irrelevance, have retarded progress: take an example of an advance dependent on animal experiments and detail how an alternative procedure could have provided the same material benefit. A suitable example would be treatment of the cardiac condition known as mitral valve insufficiency, caused by a defect in the heart's mitral valve. The production of prosthetic heart valves stemmed from years of development and testing for efficacy in dogs and calves. The artificial valve can be inserted only into a quiescent heart that has been bypassed by a heart-lung machine—an instrument that itself has been perfected after 20 years' experimentation in dogs. If, despite the benefit of 35 years of hindsight, critics of animal research cannot present a convincing scenario to show how effective treatment of mitral valve insufficiency could have developed any other way, their credibility is suspect.

Will animal experiments continue to be necessary to resolve extant medical problems? Transgenic animals with a single mutant gene have already provided a wealth of new information on the functions of proteins and their roles in disease; no doubt they will continue to do so. We also anticipate major progress in the treatment of traumatic injury to the central nervous system. The dogma that it is impossible to restore function to damaged nerve cells in the mammalian spinal cord has to be reassessed in the light of recent animal research indicating that nerve regeneration is indeed possible. It is only a matter of time before treatments begin to work. We find it difficult to envision how progress in this field—and so many others in biological and medical science—can be achieved in the future without animal experiments.

# Animal-to-Human Organ Transplants Could Benefit Humans

**by John J. Fung**

**About the author:** *John J. Fung is the chief of transplantation at the University of Pittsburg Medical Center.*

With the success of human-to-human transplantation, the need for organ replacement has grown to critical levels. (An estimated 65,000 Americans suffering from end-stage organ failure currently are awaiting organ transplantation and the number is growing each year.) The demand for organs has inspired concerted research efforts in the field of xenotransplantation—the use of animal organs as replacements for human organs. Nearly 5,000 people die each year because suitable donors are not found in time, so any progress toward expanding the pool of organs—including the use of animal organs—has implications that literally translate into human lives.

## Ending the Suffering

Despite heightened public awareness to address the need for organ donation, there appears to be little prospect of increasing supplies to meet current shortages satisfactorily. The ability to use animal organs successfully as permanent replacements for failing human organs would end the suffering and death of patients awaiting transplantation. (More than 10% of patients awaiting transplantation die each year because of lack of human organs.) While artificial organs may become a reality with future developments, their ability to replace complex organs, such as the liver, is likely to be years away. Recent developments in understanding the barriers to successful xenotransplantation, along with access to novel drugs and approaches to manipulate the immune system, are making xenotransplantation more clinically feasible and bringing it much closer to reality.

Case reports of using animal kidneys appeared in the early 1900s from

John J. Fung, "Transplanting Animal Organs into Humans Is Feasible," *USA Today*, vol. 128, November 1999, p. 54. Copyright © 1999 by Society for the Advancement of Education. Reproduced by permission.

sources including pigs, goats, nonhuman primates, and lambs, but they met with failure, as did the earliest attempts at human-to-human transplantation. In the 1960s, a number of nonhuman primate-to-human kidney transplants were attempted, due to the pressing need for organs prior to the adoption of legislation that defined brain death and allowed cadaveric donation. Even with relatively ineffective forms of immunosuppression, function of non-human primate xenografts could be demonstrated, in one patient up to nine months after transplantation of a chimpanzee kidney.

In 1963, seven patients received baboon kidneys, all of which functioned immediately. These xenografts maintained dialysis-free function for up to 60 days before failing from rejection. With advances in immunosuppression and facing a severe shortage of pediatric donor hearts, Dr. Leonard Bailey transplanted a baboon heart into "Baby Fae" in 1983. Although that immunosuppressive regimen included cyclosporine, a new antirejection drug widely used today, the heart was eventually rejected 20 days after transplantation. No further attempts at xenotransplantation were done for almost a decade, until three attempts at liver xenotransplantation were reported between 1992 and 1993.

> ***"The ability to use animal organs successfully . . . would end the suffering and death of patients awaiting transplantation."***

When organs are transplanted across closely related species (e.g., baboon to human), such xenotransplants are referred to as "concordant." On the other hand, organs transplanted across widely divergent species (e.g., pig to human) are termed "discordant." These terms characterize the extent of difficulty that exists in striving for successful organ transplantation across these barriers. It is much easier to achieve xenograft acceptance across concordant than discordant combinations. Chimpanzees are considered the most biologically superior donor because they are genetically the closest to humans, but their threat of extinction precludes their use. Baboons, while not as similar to humans as chimpanzees, can be easily raised in captivity and are not an endangered species.

## Pig Potential

Pigs are available in sufficient quantities, have similar anatomy and physiology to humans, and can be bred under conditions in which they can be genetically modified. While these factors have prompted the consideration of this species as a source for clinical xenotransplantation, organs from discordant species are confronted with a formidable barrier—almost immediate rejection within minutes mediated by naturally occurring antibodies (also called preformed xenoantibodies) which are present in the recipient. Because of the difficulty in controlling such rejection (also known as hyperacute rejection), novel approaches are required to overcome this barrier to successful discordant xenotransplantation.

All humans have preformed antibodies to pig tissue, which would lead to hyperacute rejection of the transplanted xenograft. However, genetically modifying pigs—in essence, "humanizing" them—shows promise in preventing such a virulent rejection from taking place. A number of biotechnology companies and a handful of universities, including the University of Pittsburgh Medical Center, are taking a closer look at the potential this approach may yield for patients awaiting lifesaving organ transplants.

## A Controversial Field

What about the controversies surrounding the field of xenotransplantation? These are extensions of debates regarding broader issues of health care, biomedical research, organ transplantation, and human experimentation. The most recent discussions have focused on the possibility that infections from the donor would be transmitted to the human species. In the broadest sense, concern has been raised for society as a whole. It is the limited availability of data on the transfer of animal-derived, infectious pathogens to humans via xenotransplantation that has endangered the debate among scientists, physicians, regulatory agencies, and public representatives.

The scenario of unleashing a "doomsday" infectious agent on the human species has been forwarded by those who have urged a moratorium on xenotransplantation. The possibility of transmission of infectious agents following xenotransplantation certainly exists, since animals harbor infectious agents—such as bacteria, fungus, and parasites—that are known pathogens. These agents can be screened for, and, in most situations, effective therapy is available. Much less is known about the natural behavior of many human and animal viruses, let alone their singular or coexistent behavior in an organ recipient whose immune system is suppressed by the drugs needed to prevent organ rejection. Nevertheless, it is somewhat comforting that studies of diabetic patients who received pig pancreatic islet cells between four and seven years ago have had no evidence of pig-derived retroviruses, suggesting that the risk of this type of infection in these patients is small.

Nevertheless, it is the "unknown" agent that imparts caution in these trials. These unknown agents are either those that have not yet been identified or more hypothetically (and thus even scarier) "mutant" pathogens that might result from genetic recombination of human and animal viruses. This issue has been especially highlighted, in light of the putative origin of the human immunodeficiency virus (HIV), thought to arise from non-human primate cells.

***"Chimpanzees are considered the most biologically superior donor."***

In the past few years, the Food and Drug Administration, the Centers for Disease Control, and the National Institutes of Health have carefully reviewed the issues surrounding xenotransplantation. In early 1998, a special symposium was convened to develop guidelines for xenotransplantation trials. This conference called for the creation of a national Xenotransplantation Advisory Committee—comprised of scientists, physicians, ethicists, lawyers, and public representatives—to review public safety issues, using guidelines established by the transplant community for monitoring of infectious complications following clinical xenotransplant efforts. In addition, recommendations were made regarding the makeup of investigative teams at specialized centers that planned to embark on xenotransplantation trials.

***"The criticism surrounding xenotransplantation is strongly reminiscent of that leveled against human-to-human transplantation."***

The criticism surrounding xenotransplantation is strongly reminiscent of that leveled against human-to-human transplantation in the late 1960s and early 1970s. Yet, with persistence, the field of human-to-human transplantation has proven highly successful. This was the result of stepwise increases in understanding of the biology of rejection, improvements in drug management, and experience. Despite the resources that have been expended in efforts to promote human organ donations and given the unlikelihood of societal acceptance of mandated donation, the rationale for pursuing xenotransplantation as a solution to the organ shortage is compelling.

It is possible that xenotransplantation may not be universally successful until further technological advances occur, yet cautious exploration of xenotransplantation appears warranted, in order to identify those areas that require further study. Technological advances and better screening tools are likely to identify donors that may harbor latent infections or allow design of genetically engineered animals that may not be as susceptible to rejection or free from infectious risks. In addition, the principles learned from these early clinical cases possibly to utilize animal organs because of their innate resistance to infection or to peculiar species-specific metabolic pathways some day may lead to functional "cures" for diseases that prove resistant to other medical or surgical therapies. The use of animal organs may be the only way we can save more lives.

# Animal Drug Tests Do Not Benefit Humans

**by C. Ray Greek and Jean Swingle Greek**

**About the author:** *C. Ray Greek is a board-certified anesthesiologist, and Jean Swingle Greek is a veterinary dermatologist. They speak at national and international forums on the subject of animal experimentation and have recently established Americans For Medical Advancement, a nonprofit foundation based in Los Angeles.*

Most medications derive from one big contradiction: Our government demands that we test all medications on animals prior to continuing to human trials, and it admits that applying animal data to humans is a "leap of faith." No wonder, then, that each year tens of thousands of people get sick from legal pharmaceuticals. And many of them die. And no wonder our diseases go uncured.

## Two Tangibles

The government's requirement yields only two tangibles—a very accurate picture of the compounds' effect on lab animals, whether positive or negative, and a legal safe harbor for the government and drug companies. When drugs cause illness and death in humans and there is an inquiry, all those involved in development and approval of the drug can point to copious animal testing and claim due diligence. The animal testing provides no surety whatsoever about what these chemicals do to humans. Even those in favor of the animal model are wary. In fact, the most widely respected textbook on the animal experimentation subject, the *Handbook on Laboratory Animal Science*, itself states,

> Uncritical reliance on the results of animal tests can be dangerously misleading and has cost the health and lives of tens of thousands of humans.

And human trials are still necessary. Those who say we test on animals to avoid testing on people are wrong. Once animal studies are complete, all new medications are evaluated on humans. The first people to take a new substance are being

C. Ray Greek and Jean Swingle Greek, *Sacred Cows and Golden Geese: The Human Cost of Experiments on Animals*. New York: Continuum, 2000. Copyright © 2000 by C. Ray Greek, MD, and Jean Swingle Greek, DVM. All rights reserved. Reproduced by permission.

experimented on as surely as if they were guinea pigs locked in a laboratory.

Open up a rat, a dog, a pig, and a human, and you will find much the same terrain but with differences. These visible differences have an impact when it comes to assimilating drugs. Consider the most commonly used species in toxicology research, the rat. Rats have no gall bladder. They excrete bile very effectively. Many drugs are excreted via bile so this affects the half-life of the drug. Drugs bind to rat plasma much less efficiently. Rats always breathe through the nose. Because some chemicals are absorbed in the nose, some are filtered. So rats get a different mix of substances entering their systems. Also they are nocturnal. Their gut flora are in a different location. Their skin has different absorptive properties than that of humans. Any one of these discrepancies will alter drug metabolism. And these are only differences on a gross level.

***"Until animals manifest grand scale malaise in a lab, observations are all guesswork."***

Smaller differences, being largely chemical, are more difficult to observe. Therein lies a greater dilemma. Medications do not act on the macro-organism—the large, visible level of, say, keeping organs in the right arrangement or bones in the right place. Medications act on the microscopic level. They interrupt and/or initiate chemical reactions, altering molecular activities that are far too small for the human eye to observe. Indeed, medications' actions are not apparent, even with high-tech instrumentation, until they occur.

The discrepancies between diverse mammals are largely microscopic. Imponderably intricate, they are born of millions of years of speciation, adaptation, and mutation. The more modern science reveals about genes, cell function, ion channels, proteins, and so on, the more apparent is the complex gulf between species. And the more ludicrous the existing requirement for animal testing becomes.

## Communication Problems

The other, even more obvious, problem with the animal model is that animals cannot communicate about their well-being. They cannot say, "I have a stomachache" or "my head hurts," or even "I ache all over." Hence, until animals manifest grand scale malaise in a lab, observations are all guesswork. Or as experts in toxicity write,

> The only universal model for a human—that is, one which would best predict what would happen at a given endpoint across the full range of chemical structures, concentrations, etc.—is other humans.

Is it possible that we are not only receiving inaccurate data about the side effects of medications, but also not receiving access to certain drugs that do not produce those side effects that animal models claim? Are we missing good medications because of animal testing? Logic suggests that the answer to these questions is *yes*.

As it is now, animal testing for medications has created and continues to create catastrophe. Animal experiments fail to predict the lethal side effects of many drugs and also prevent good medications from reaching the marketplace. These two outcomes are called "false negatives" and "false positives," as we will explain. The critical word here is false. Animal models for human medicine are false.

Different chemicals have diverse effects on different species. Therefore, the belief that "simply doing enough animal testing will predict all human toxicity" is, as Dr. Louis Lasagna of the University of Rochester so eloquently put it, a "pathetic illusion."

When compounds demonstrate therapeutic effect on an animal, therapeutic effect without ill side effect, they proceed to human clinical trials. There, very often—our research shows anywhere from 52 to 100 percent of the time—they fail, frequently by wounding or killing people. Animal testing has made it look as if given compounds will not injure humans, but they do. Test results such as these are called "false negatives," an important term in the trial process. Thalidomide [which caused birth defects when taken by pregnant women but showed no side effects in animals] is a perfect example of a false negative.

The second catastrophic impact of animal testing is this: compounds that show evidence of therapeutic effect in the human arena are tested on animals. When they bring on injurious side effects in animals, they are withheld from development for humans. More people stay ill. More people die. When it later turns out that humans do not experience the side effects as animals did and also that they actually benefit from the medication, then the animal modeled test results are called "false positives"—a second significant drawback to the animal testing protocol. . . .

***"Animal testing for medications has created . . . catastrophe."***

## Cures Worse than Illness

Ushering drugs to market through animal testing is treacherous. Legal drugs kill more people per year than all illegal drugs combined. An article from an April 1998 *Journal of the American Medical Association* described a study that concluded that deaths from adverse reactions to medications are the fourth leading killer of Americans. (This study's findings are controversial and should not be misinterpreted as condemning all medications, but suffice it to say that medications are killing many patients.) In 1994 adverse drug reactions killed an estimated 106,000 Americans. It is well accepted that approximately 100,000 deaths per year and approximately fifteen percent of all hospital admissions are caused by adverse medication reactions. This costs the general public over $136 billion annually.

As noted, thalidomide is but one high profile disaster. In fact, medical history is strewn with comparable hazardous medications and human fatalities—all traceable to drug development's dependency on the animal model.

The following short histories begin to suggest how drastically human physiology differs from that of lab animals used by pharmaceutical companies in drug development. . . .

- Rexar, an antibiotic, was withdrawn by Glaxo as it had been linked with severe cardiovascular events and seven deaths.
- Celebrex, an arthritis drug, a COX-2 inhibitor, was linked to ten deaths and eleven cases of GI [gastrointestinal] hemorrhage in its first three months on the market.
- Zimeldine, the first SSRI (selective serotonin reuptake inhibitor), caused a paralyzing illness known as Guillain-Barre syndrome, not predicted by animal tests, and was withdrawn. This delayed the marketing of Prozac, which proved safe.
- Enbrel (etanercept), a treatment for rheumatoid arthritis, has been associated with serious infections and deaths. The manufacturer, Immunex, is relabeling the drug.
- Zafirlukast (Accolate), a common medication used to treat asthma, has recently been linked, by human studies, to a rare and sometimes fatal condition known as Churg-Strauss syndrome. Despite extensive testing on animals, this complication did not manifest until Accolate was released to the general public. If larger clinical trials were mandatory, perhaps like situations would not arise.
- Birth control pills, as we now know, can cause life threatening blood clots in some women. To the best of our knowledge, scientists have still not been able to reproduce this finding in animals, certainly not for lack of trying! Extensive animal tests revealed no such problem. In fact, dog testing predicted that the pill would actually decrease the likelihood of clotting. Scientists said this about the animal studies of birth control pills:

> [Of] the conditions in humans associated epidemiologically with an increased risk in pill users . . . none . . . was predicted by toxicity tests in experimental animals . . . The increase risk of thromboembolic disorders [stroke], which is primarily associated with the estrogen component of the pill, has no analogue in animals. Changes in blood coagulation parameters have only been observed in dogs, but in them they have been due to a specific progestin-related increase in plasma fibrinogen. . . . It is apparent that most of the salient findings in animal experiments have lacked analogues in humans, and most of the adverse and beneficial effects associated with the use of contraceptives have not been predicted by toxicity tests. . . .

## Misguided Development

How did scientists learn that these drugs were murderous? Not through animal testing. Epidemiology, clinical observation, and autopsy proved these medications were deleterious. The ill effects of using diethylene glycol as an ingredient in medications were found by autopsy and epidemiology. The complications of phenacetin causing necrotizing papillitis and interstitial nephritis; the anesthetic halothane causing liver damage; zoxazolamine (a muscle relaxant) causing lethal liver disease; the complications of chemotherapy, and many more problems manifested through autopsy and clinical observation.

***"Ushering drugs to market through animal testing is treacherous."***

A book like Stephen Fried's *Bitter Pills* [an investigation into the international pharmaceutical industry] could be built around any one of the drugs above. All had misguided development. All were envisioned as highly profitable. All banked on Americans' trust in the medical profession and its adjunct, the pharmaceutical industry. All destroyed not just one or two people's lives, but many lives. Our list leaves these personal tragedies undescribed, but emphasizes instead the magnitude of the problem the animal model creates. . . .

## Delusions of Harm

"Normally, animal experiments not only fail to contribute to the safety of medications, but they even have the opposite effect." So stated Dr. Kurt Fickentscher of the Pharmacological Institute of the University of Bonn, Germany, in *Diagnosen*, March 1980. Here is another scientist emphasizing that animal tests not only fail to predict the bad effects. When they falsely predict side effects, it keeps good medications off the market. [Researchers] T. Koppanyi and M.A. Avery stated of many medications that are used to save lives today, "Had these drugs first been tested in animal experiments for their safety, some of them might never have reached clinical trial." The truth is that all medications in use today can be found to cause a serious side effect in some animal. *Given that, if medications were withheld based on a negative side effect in animals, we would have no medications today.*

Pharmaceutical companies are very wary of releasing drugs that have extremely negative effects on their test animals for legal reasons. Therefore, they keep some of these compounds off the market. Again, as explained earlier, when an animal experiment predicts side effects that do not occur in humans, it is called a "false positive." It is the false positives that prevent potentially therapeutic medications from reaching afflicted humans who really need them.

For an idea of just how helpful these medications might be, we have only to weigh the personal benefit of several common painkillers—drugs that demonstrate false positives in animals but have outstanding therapeutic value in the human setting.

Look in your own medicine cabinet. When you get a headache, would you reach for a pain medication of which a single dose causes renal failure and death in cats? Perhaps. That medication is acetaminophen most commonly marketed as Tylenol. Leery now of Tylenol, you might prefer aspirin. Today, twenty-nine billion aspirin per year are sold in the United States and twice that number are sold worldwide. Aspirin is not only used for pain relief and fever reduction but for the prevention of strokes, heart attacks, and other illnesses. Aspirin causes birth defects in mice and rats and results in such extensive blood abnormalities in cats that they can only take twenty percent of the human dosage every third day. How about ibuprofen, which most people know as Advil or Motrin? Ibuprofen causes kidney failure in dogs, even at very low doses. . . .

***"'Animal experiments . . . fail to contribute to the safety of medications.'"***

## Examples of False Positives

We found many other examples of valuable medications of which Americans were initially deprived because the mandate for animal testing prevents their development and distribution here.

- Depo-Provera, the contraceptive, was barred from release in the U.S. in 1973 because it caused cancer in dogs and baboons. Elsewhere in the world, women used it and found it safe. Not until 1993 did the FDA release the drug to the American public.
- Digitalis, a plant used by herbalists for centuries to treat heart disorders, was discovered without animal use. However, clinical trials of the drug were delayed when it caused high blood pressure in animals. Digoxin, an analogue of digitalis, was much later released and has saved countless lives. How many more could it have saved had it been released sooner?
- Streptomycin, a popular antibiotic, is teratogenic in rats, causing limb malformations in offspring. . . .
- Furosemide, commonly called Lasix, is another example of an important medication almost lost to the public due to animal studies. It is a diuretic, used to treat high blood pressure and heart disease. Mice, rats and hamsters suffer liver damage from this widely used drug, but people do not. The drug is metabolized differently in each species.
- Fluoride, which causes cancer in rats, was initially withheld from dental use. A dentist made the discovery that fluoride may decrease the risk of dental decay. Observing patients who had mottled teeth from living in areas with a large concentration of fluoride in the water, he noticed that they had fewer cavities. . . .

## Searching for Side Effects

All medications in use today can cause a serious side effect in some animal. As we have already explained, if researchers persevere, inculcating enough species with high enough dosages, illness will eventually result in one or more species. Hence, if we truly withheld any medication from the public based on its negative impact on non-humans, we would have no medications today. This fact alone destroys all justification for continuing animal testing.

The more we learn in regard to the physiological differences between humans and other animals, the more strained support for animal experimentation becomes. What use are animal tests if scientists' chances of predicting safety are no better than fifty percent? The troubled impact of the animal model on drugs covered in this [viewpoint] albeit incomplete, is tragic enough to merit overhaul of drug development procedures.

# Animal-to-Human Organ Transplants Could Threaten Human Health

**by Jonathan Hughes**

**About the author:** *Jonathan Hughes is a lecturer in political thought in the department of government at the University of Manchester.*

The idea of using animals as a source of organs for transplant into humans [known as xenotransplantation] has been around for some time, but until now these procedures have been bedevilled by problems of immune system rejection: few patients have survived more than a few weeks and many have died in a matter of hours or less. Recently, however, there has been an upsurge of interest, resulting from technological developments that offer improved prospects for xenograft recipients. Better immunosuppressive drugs may help to reduce the rate of rejection, particularly with organs from closely related species such as baboons, and genetic modification of donor animals (particularly pigs) may improve their organs' compatibility with human recipients and hence reduce human immune system responses. . . .

In exploring [the ethical issues surrounding xenotransplantation] it will be argued that although the 1997 reports for the Nuffield Council on Bioethics and the Department of Health have made important contributions to this debate, both reach conclusions that are insufficiently cautious in the light of the problems that they address. . . .

## The Risk of Epidemics

The most important [ethical] issues here are the risk that diseases transmitted from animals to humans may prove infectious between humans, leading perhaps to new AIDS-type epidemics, and the costs that will be borne by other patients if resources are redirected from other areas of medical research and treatment to fund xenotransplantation. The fact that xenotransplantation carries risks not just

Jonathan Hughes, "Xenografting: Ethical Issues," *Journal of Medical Ethics*, vol. 24, February 1998, pp. 18–24. Copyright © 1998 by the BJM Publishing Group. Reproduced by permission.

for the xenograft recipient but for the population generally is important because it takes the ethics of xenotransplantation outside the realm of individual consent and into the realm of *justice*, raising questions about the extent to which it is permissible for an individual to impose risks on others for his own benefit.

The issue of reallocating resources is not specific to xenotransplantation, but raises the same problems as the introduction of any other new and experimental treatment—problems of predicting future costs and benefits and of ensuring effective and equitable use of resources. The question here is whether xenotransplantation would be a better or worse use of resources than the available alternatives.

## Calculating Risks

The risk of transmitting infectious diseases to the wider population, however, is an altogether more serious problem. We do accept the imposition of some risks on others for our own benefit (for example when we drive cars). However, there are limits to what we regard as acceptable (it is not acceptable, for example, to drive when drunk), and it is therefore necessary to consider the nature of the risk imposed on the wider population by xenotransplantation procedures. The difficulty for proponents of xenotransplantation is that the worst-case scenario (a major new epidemic) is extremely grave, and its likelihood is difficult if not impossible to quantify. As the Nuffield report explains:

> It will be very difficult to identify organisms that do not cause any symptoms in the animal from which they come. Previous experience indicates that infectious organisms are normally identified only after the emergence of the disease they cause. . . . Put bluntly, it may be possible to identify any infectious organism transmitted by xenografting only if it causes disease in human beings, and after it has started to do so.

Moreover, if, as in the case of HIV, there is a long incubation period between infection and development of the disease, the agent may have spread far beyond the original xenograft recipient by the time its symptoms are noticed, undermining any hope of containing the infection. The Nuffield report concludes from these considerations that the risk of a major epidemic is unquantifiable, and in the light of this advocates a *precautionary principle*, requiring "that action should be taken to avoid risks *in advance* of certainty about their nature" and that "the burden of proof should lie with those developing the technology to demonstrate that it will not cause serious harm". Unfortunately, the measures that the report proposes in order to safeguard against disease transmission do not live up to this principle.

> ***"The difficulty for proponents of xenotransplantation is that the worst-case scenario (a major new epidemic) is extremely grave."***

The report begins robustly enough, by stating:

> that the risks associated with possible transmission of infectious diseases as a consequence of xenotransplantation have not been adequately dealt with. It would not be ethical, therefore to begin clinical trials of xenotransplantation involving human beings.

## Precautions Are Not Watertight

However, the report goes on to suggest that xenotransplantation should be allowed to proceed once the following conditions have been satisfied: (1) that "as much information as possible" be assembled about the risks of transmission; (2) that source animals be "reared in conditions in which all known infectious organisms are monitored and controlled"; (3) that early recipients undergo regular monitoring and testing; and (4) that there be "a commitment to suspend, modify or, if necessary, discontinue xenotransplantation procedures at any signs that new infectious diseases are emerging". These precautions, however, are far from watertight, for, as noted above, the report acknowledges that *full* knowledge of potentially ineffective agents is for all practical purposes impossible. A consequence of this is that source animals cannot be freed from *all* infectious organisms but only those that are known and can be reliably tested for: "Specified pathogen-free animals may still be infected with unidentified infectious organisms about which nothing is known". Because the risk of disease transmission cannot be eliminated, the report recommends that procedures for monitoring of recipients be established and that consent to this be included in consent to the xenograft. Monitoring, however, is of no use unless backed-up by a plan of action, and as the following passage demonstrates, the report fails utterly to provide such a plan.

> ***"Source animals cannot be freed from* all *infectious organisms."***

> The most difficult question is what procedure should be followed if it is found that a disease has indeed been transmitted from the animals used to provide organs or tissue to human xenograft recipients? In principle, steps should be taken to prevent transmission of the disease to other people. In practice, this is a very difficult issue. For a start, it is very unlikely that, at the outset, the mode of transmission of the disease will be understood. The appropriate response will depend on the mode of transmission and on how infectious the disease is. It would hardly be acceptable to isolate xenograft recipients suffering from an infectious disease, or to ask them to refrain from sexual intercourse or, in the case of a virus transmitted from parent to offspring, from having children. This highlights how difficult it would be to prevent the transmission of an infectious disease originating from xenotransplantation. It is sobering to reflect on the difficulty, despite globally coordinated attempts, of controlling and eliminating infectious diseases such as malaria, hepatitis and AIDS.

This is indeed a sobering passage, and given such pessimism about the prospects for containment of any new infection, the precautionary principle would appear to require that the proposed moratorium on xenotransplantation procedures be made indefinite.

The Department of Health report goes further than the Nuffield report in discriminating the risks posed by different kinds of infectious agents, but reaches similar conclusions. Fungi, parasites and bacteria, it concludes, pose relatively little risk either to the xenograft recipient or to the wider population. With regard to prions, it holds that transmission to xenograft recipients is unlikely (though recent controversy about the transmissibility of prion disease from BSE-infected cattle [cattle with bovine spongiform encephalopathy, a fatal disease commonly called mad cow disease] to humans might lead us to doubt the reliability of scientific advice on this matter), and that prions are unlikely to be transmitted from one human to another. In view of the latter, the long incubation period typical of prion disease appears as an advantage rather than a disadvantage, allowing that even an infected recipient may benefit from years of good quality life, without posing a risk to others. The greatest risk, the report concludes, is from viruses, due to their transmissibility between humans, the long incubation periods of some viral infections, and our limited ability to screen for and exclude known and unknown viruses in donor animals. As far as viruses are concerned, the Department of Health report concurs with the Nuffield report that the risk of infection and onward transmission is at present too great to justify experimental procedures.

## A Moratorium Should Be Imposed

Unfortunately the Department of Health report runs into the same difficulties as the Nuffield report in considering the future conditions under which xenografting might become acceptable. It too premises the future acceptability of xenotransplantation upon the hope that further research may show the risk of infection to be "within tolerable margins", while acknowledging that it cannot ever be totally ruled out. In expressing this hope, however, the report ignores the difficulty, raised by the Nuffield report, of quantifying, and assessing as tolerable, a risk posed by agents that are as yet unidentified. The Department of Health report also follows the Nuffield report in advocating monitoring of xenograft recipients as a further safeguard against the spreading of infections and, again, like the Nuffield report, offers no satisfactory account of what should be done in the event of a positive result, suggesting only that "appropriate additional research" may be indicated. . . .

A moratorium should be imposed upon xenotransplantation procedures at least until possible avenues for increasing the supply of human organs have been exhausted and until a more reassuring judgment can be reached on the prospects for preventing and containing transmitted infections.

Chapter 3

# Should Animals Be Bred for Human Consumption?

# Chapter Preface

At the heart of the question of whether animals should be raised for human consumption is the issue of corporate-run meat operations. Confined Animal Feeding Operations (CAFOs), or factory farms, have become the dominant method of raising meat in America. Factory farms are livestock operations in which enormous numbers of food animals are bred and raised. The animals are typically kept in small, indoor enclosures until they are taken to the slaughterhouse. According to many animal rights activists, factory farming is a cruel way to raise animals for human consumption. In Defense of Animals, a national animal rights organization, states, "A majority of the animals that are raised for food live miserable lives in intensive confinement in dark, overcrowded facilities."

Factory farming began in the 1920s with the discovery of vitamins A and D. Farmers realized that when they added the vitamins to animals' feed, the animals no longer needed exercise and sunlight for growth. This discovery permitted farmers to raise large numbers of animals indoors year-round. The only problem they encountered with the new system was how quickly animals in such close quarters spread disease; the problem was solved with the development of antibiotics in the 1940s. Technological advances in machinery and assembly-line techniques permitted farmers to increase productivity and decrease costs.

This system of mass production, according to animal rights activists, has unfortunately resulted in the misery and suffering of millions of animals. Animals raised in CAFOs have had their genes manipulated and are inundated with antibiotics, hormones, and other chemicals to produce large quantities of meat as quickly as possible. Chickens, for example, are selectively bred and genetically altered to produce larger breasts and thighs, the cuts most in demand. The birds grow so heavy that their legs and feet cannot support their bodies, resulting in broken bones and painful deformations. Moreover, according to one agricultural journal, "[chickens] now grow so rapidly that the heart and lungs are not developed well enough to support the remainder of the body, resulting in congestive heart failure and tremendous death losses." The chickens are crowded in enormous battery cages where they have less than half a square foot of space per bird. The birds frequently have their beaks clipped and their toes removed to minimize fighting with the other birds. Supporters of animal rights contend that these conditions are cruel and cause chickens to suffer unnecessarily.

Chickens are not the only animals that endure deplorable living conditions, according to animal rights advocates. Pigs, as stated by the organization Farm Sanctuary, "are being treated more as inanimate tools of production than as living, feeling animals." Piglets are subjected to painful mutilations without anesthesia. Their tails are cut off to minimize tail biting, an aberrant behavior that pigs demonstrate when they are unnaturally confined, and their ears are notched for identification. After they are weaned, the pigs are packed into pens with metal bars and concrete floors where they live until they are slaughtered at about six months of age. Animal rights supporters maintain that lack of exercise and hard flooring results in obesity and crippling leg injuries. A recent study on the effects of confinement on pigs found that "scientific evidence suggests that intensive confinement causes both physical and psychological disorders in [pigs]."

As a result of increasing awareness of the conditions in which factory farm animals live, animal activists have pushed for more humane methods of raising animals for food. Small independent farmers have begun to produce poultry, beef, pork, and eggs on traditional pasture farms that do not confine animals to inadequate cages. Pasture farms allow animals to graze and roam freely. Pasture-farm products are more expensive than corporate products, but animal rights advocates claim that supporting humane methods of raising animals for food is worth the extra cost. The best way to reduce the misery suffered by factory farm animals, in the opinion of animal rights supporters, is to purchase pasture-raised animal products instead of factory-raised products. The authors in the following chapter debate pasture farms as well as other issues related to the raising of animals for human consumption.

# A Case for Meat-Eating

**by Colin Tudge**

**About the author:** *Colin Tudge is a three-time winner of the Glaxo/ABSW Science Writer of the Year Award. His career as a science writer includes serving as Features Editor at* New Scientist, *his own science program,* Spectrum, *on BBC Radio, and freelance writing for the* Independent, *the* Times, Natural History *and the* New Statesman.

The roast beef of England has been consumed by the fire of spring; April [2001] has indeed proved the cruellest month. My local butcher, an excellent man but of a dying breed, tells me that he is having a very bad time. People don't seem to catch foot-and-mouth-disease (there has been just one, somewhat equivocal case—but they said that about BSE [bovine spongiform encephalopathy], didn't they?), yet many now find themselves repelled by meat. Have the vegetarians been right all along? Should we consign carnivory to our barbarous past? Would it not be safer for each of us, individually, to become vegetarian? And good for the planet as a whole? Was BSE the portent, and FMD the coup de grace?[1]

It is a close-run thing, but on balance the answer is no. Animal husbandry all over the world, when done well, is good and necessary. The arguments for vegetarianism don't quite work.

But they are certainly salutary. Modern livestock production really must mend its ways, for the epidemics are indeed an outrage. And while vegetarians are not quite equipped to take over the world, they do form a stout opposition. If farming is Greek tragedy (and the resemblance grows month by month with the hubris), then the veggies are the necessary Furies.

## Win Some, Lose Some

In terms of nutrition, vegetarians have won most of the battles, though they have lost some along the way: when Percy Bysshe Shelley gave up meat, he be-

1. In 2000 an outbreak of bovine spongiform encephalopathy (BSE), or mad cow disease, began in England and spread throughout Europe. Some of the people who ate the infected beef developed Creutzfeld-Jakob disease, a variant of BSE that infects humans. Foot-and-mouth disease is a viral infection that targets cloven-hoofed animals and poses no risk to humans.

Colin Tudge, "Should The World Renounce Meat?" *New Statesman*, vol. 130, April 30, 2001, p. 27.
Copyright © 2001 by New Statesman, Ltd. Reproduced by permission.

came even more languid than usual, until his unlikely friend Thomas Love Peacock recommended "three mutton chops with pepper". For most of the 20th century, protein seemed the main issue. Nutritionists in John Steinbeck's *Tortilla Flat*, written in 1935, wondered how a local Mexican boy flourished on an apparently exclusive diet of tortillas and frijoles. Their theory told them that neither maize (cereal) nor beans (pulses) contain enough protein to keep a gnat on its trembling feet, yet this presumptuous lad seemed bright as a button. Clearly, they concluded, he must be some kind of changeling. A freak of nature. It never occurred to them, as good scientists, to question their own theory.

But Steinbeck was a biologist manque and his anecdote was rooted in contemporary thinking. Notably, in the early 1930s, [noted nutritionist and pediatrician] Cicely Williams suggested after preliminary studies in Africa that kwashiorkor, the strange pot-bellied syndrome that afflicts many children suffering malnutrition, resulted not from a lack of food in general, but specifically from a deficiency of protein. In the middle decades of the 20th century, this became the dogma (even though some brave souls were questioning it by the early 1950s).

Protein seemed to mean meat, eggs, milk, and then more of the same, which suited the newly invigorated, newly bullish agriculture of postwar Britain and the US: meat removes the ceiling on turnover, and is the key to riches. Commerce, nutritional theory and hedonism (because people like meat) marched precisely in step, which is rarely the case. Meat was marketed as keenly as Craven A cigarettes and nylons, and yet had virtue on its side. A fine American academic, Georg Borgstrom, wrote a book in the 1960s to prove that most of humanity must already be dead, since they were clearly protein-deficient.

## Protein-Sparing

The tide truly turned in the 1970s, on three fronts. First, protein ceased to be the elixir. The concept of "protein-sparing" came to the fore. Williams was right: the kwashiorkor children were protein-deficient. But that was not because their diet lacked protein. It lacked energy, and their desperate bodies, needing to survive second by second, "burned" precious protein to supply it.

Energy could be supplied much more cheaply, and for the body more easily, by carbohydrate—starch—or fat. This would then "spare" the protein. Nutritionists now vied with each other to reduce the recommended daily dose. Suddenly, and with wondrous serendipity, all the great staples emerged as adequate sources of protein: pulses, cereals, even potatoes. People can live almost exclusively on potatoes. As a final bonus, pulse protein makes good any deficiency in cereal protein, so that frijoles and tortillas (or dhal and chapatti or beans on toast) make a perfect match.

> ***"The arguments for vegetarianism don't quite work."***

This "paradigm shift" was perhaps the most significant revelation of the 20th century, because it implied, after all, that humanity could feed itself. But there was more, for nutritionists also began at last to accept that dietary fibre, hitherto disdained as "roughage", was in various ways auspicious, not to say vital—and fibre is supplied by plants. Finally, and most conspicuously, people grew worried by saturated fat, which is mainly the domain of animal flesh, and enthused by unsaturates—for example, from sunflowers (polyunsaturated) and olives (monounsaturated).

> ***"Some minerals . . . are hard to guarantee without animal products."***

Nutritionally, however, animal food still has much to offer—particularly for poorer people, or in far-flung places, without access to vegetables of excellent quality or to a health-food shop. Some minerals, notably zinc and calcium, are hard to guarantee without animal products. Parts of animals also supply recondite "essential fats", which perhaps are of particular importance for the development of nerves and brains. In many countries—in semideserts and high latitudes—it is far easier to produce livestock than to grow reliable crops; so animals become prime sources of both protein and energy. In all countries, animal products are good nutritional underwriters—good guarantors of quality. Peacock's instincts were spot on.

## Defining Animal Products

"Animal products" should be defined broadly, however: to include the trotters and offal that were once part of every traditional cuisine. The supermarkets' dedication to steaks and cutlets, profitable though this may be, is nutritionally pernicious. And animal products should not be eaten in vast amounts. Great cuisines use meat as garnish; it becomes the centrepiece only on feast days. Excess is vulgar, to say the least, as any vegetarian would attest. Still, a low-meat diet is better than a no-meat diet.

It is not true—or not as true as they would like it to be—that vegetarians have no blood on their hands. It is true that modern ways of producing livestock are often disgusting. Common sense says that the battery and the intensive-care unit are cruel, and such science as there is (it is hard to find appropriate studies) supports common sense. The insouciance is increasing, too: there are "pig cities" in the US with a million desperate creatures on board. Genetic engineering is not innately evil, when tempered by aesthetics and good sense; but when applied to animals in the cause of productivity, it has proved vile—enough to give all science a bad name, as many scientists themselves point out.

But the human species cannot survive without farming, except in trivial numbers; and we cannot survive at all without encroaching on animals to some extent. Even the vegans must clear the jungle to grow their cabbages and corn. Every human being who elects to live causes at least some animals to die. Simple morality suggests—at least to a lot of people, including me—that the carnage and the suffering that we cause to animals should be minimal, and never gratuitous. I despise fox-hunting, for instance, although that is another story. Vegetarians cannot avoid the blood on their hands, but do they have less blood than the rest of us? Do they have the least that is possible?

## Degrees of Vegetarianism

Here, there is a dichotomy: between the vegans who eschew all animal products that directly involve the death of animals, including leather, and the varying shades of "lacto-ovo" vegetarians who accept milk and eggs and sometimes fish (among which, as in Japan, they sometimes classify whales). The vegans have purity on their side, and do seem to occupy high moral ground. The lacto-ovo case seems merely effete.

Lacto-vegetarians rely heavily on dairy products (which means, incidentally, that many of their most highly prized recipes are high in the dreaded saturated fat). Cows cannot lactate unless they first produce a calf, and this raises a host of practical and moral issues. Dairy cows produce one calf a year after a nine-month pregnancy. The calves are then taken away, and the cows milked for the following ten months. Thus, at any time, they are either lactating or they are heavily pregnant; for seven months of the year, they are both. Typically, in modern systems, they produce their first calf when two years old (first becoming pregnant at about 15 months), and the average age at slaughter, when they typically go for pies, is now around five years. They produce around 1,000 gallons in the ten-month lactation, although the 2,000-gallon cow is not uncommon. Not surprisingly, those with the biggest udders are prone to lameness. Wild, ancestral cows, by contrast, produce about 300 gallons a year, and may live until they are about 15. In the wild, too, cattle live in herds of about a dozen, with a recognised social hierarchy. The average modern British herd has about 100 animals—a constant crowd.

Thus the life of dairy cows is short (by cattle standards) and hard. It is becoming possible to bias the sex ratio of their calves as required, but only a few females are kept as herd replacements and the rest are killed. So are all the males. We could put the superannuated cows and their calves into retirement homes, like donkey sanctuaries. But in a few years we would need a sanctuary the size of Europe to accommodate the surplus animals from Britain's dairy herd alone, and soon after that they would occupy the whole world. Death must be built in to the system. The question is not whether but when the calves should be slaughtered.

***"The question is not whether but when the calves should be slaughtered."***

They can be kept for veal—which need not be the obscene practice it has sometimes been, if we do not insist on anaemic meat. Or, if the cow has been crossed with a beefy bull, the calves can be raised for 18 months or so and killed for beef. Most of Britain's beef comes from this source. A cow requires a huge intake of energy and hence of food to produce a calf. If the calf is simply thrown away, then the input is wasted, and such waste is surely a sin. Since slaughter is inevitable anyway, the only thrifty course is to eat the meat that results. In this, the lacto-vegetarians are on dubious moral ground indeed.

## Taking Advantage of Resources

Vegetarians also argue that an all-plant diet makes better use of landscape and resource, and hence is better for the entire planet. After all, a field laid out to wheat or potatoes yields at least ten times as much protein and energy as one devoted to cattle or sheep. Indeed so; but some fields are too steep or cold or rocky or high or marshy or dry to yield crops at all, although they might support sheep or goats. All crop production produces surpluses and leftovers, and this is the traditional domain of pigs and poultry. In short, however many crops you may fit into a given stretch of land, you can always produce even more human food if you add a few animals. The mistake is to add too many: not to complement production of cereals and pulses with livestock, but to grow them specifically to feed to livestock, which is what we do on an ever-increasing scale in the west. But again, although we see that the no-meat diet is better than the high-meat diet that has become the norm in the past half-century, it is surpassed none the less by the low-meat diet.

Finally, on the matter of morality, we might turn to [philosopher] Immanuel Kant, as doughty a court of appeal on such issues as ever there was. He suggested that no course of action can be morally unimpeachable unless it might be recommended, in principle, to everybody. Vegetarianism could not safely or responsibly be recommended to all the world's people. We in the west, who eat most meat, could indeed do without it all together. But even we would benefit from eating just a little; and there are many places without fertile plains and a forgiving climate that would be lost without it.

So while vegetarians occupy a moral high ground, they do not occupy the highest ground conceivable. They make many sound points and should be listened to. In particular, they have possibly done more than anyone to counter the hysteria of the postwar decades, when medical science and agricultural economy combined to persuade humanity as a whole that we would surely die without meat, meat, and more meat: perhaps the most pernicious piece of nonsense, both individually and globally, as can be conceived. Vegetarians have shown, after all, that with a following wind we can do without meat altogether, which is good to know.

The trick and the challenge, none the less, is not to banish animals, but to keep them properly—in proper numbers, and with due attention to their inevitable parasites. The biology is straightforward. Economics is the problem. If we want to be kind, and safe, then we must pay. And because meat shouldn't just mean steak, we must relearn how to cook.

# Pasture-Raising Animals for Human Consumption Is Beneficial

**by Jo Robinson**

**About the author:** *Jo Robinson is a* New York Times *best-selling writer and the author and publisher of* Why Grass-Fed Is Best.

Grass-fed meat and dairy products have less fat and more vitamin E, beta-carotene and cancer-fighting fatty acids than factory-farm products. All across the country, farmers and ranchers are returning to this ancient and healthier way of raising animals. Instead of sending them to feedlots to be fattened on grain, farmers are keeping animals home on the range. Cattle graze, lie down, chew their cud, graze—a soothing cycle, repeated day after day—and chickens hunt for seeds and bugs as their ancestors have for eons.

Although raising livestock on pasture is viewed as a radical departure from modern ranching, it is simply a return to a more balanced system. Ranchers boycotting the feedlots are hardworking pioneers whose goal is to make a living selling their products directly to customers or farmer's markets, restaurants and natural food stores. By eliminating some of the middlemen they hope to accomplish what can seem like an impossible dream: making a decent living from a small, family farm. Many of the ranchers have another goal, as well. In addition to feeding their families, they want to create a workable, profitable alternative to agribusiness-as-usual.

After three years of examining this grassroots movement, I've become convinced these farmers are on the right track. Raising animals on pasture is better for the animals, ranchers, environment and health of the consumer. It's one of those rare situations in life that is a win-win-win-win.

I became interested in pasture-based ranching several years ago when I was writing *The Omega Diet* with Dr. Artemis P. Simopoulos, an authority on nutrition. The book focuses on the health benefits of a Greek Mediterranean diet and

Jo Robinson, "Pasture Perfect," *Mother Earth News*, April/May 2002, p. 46. Copyright © 2002 by Ogden Publications, Inc. Reproduced by permission.

stresses the importance of eating a diet rich in omega-3 fatty acids. Omega-3s have been proven to lower the risk of a long list of diseases including cardiovascular disease, cancer, depression, allergies, auto-immune disorders, obesity and diabetes.

To get the benefits of omega-3s, most people eat fish, flaxseed, walnuts or take fish oil pills. Few realize these lifesaving fats are also found in the products of grazing animals. The reason is simple: Omega-3 fatty acids are created in the green leaves of plants, where they are essential for photosynthesis. When animals eat lots of greens they naturally accumulate more of these essential fats in their bodies. For example, steak from grass-fed cattle has two to six times more omega-3s than a steak from grain-fed cattle according to research at the University of Hawaii. When we eat the steak, the omega-3s are passed on to us.

It's often said, "We are what we eat." The truth goes deeper. We are also what our animals eat.

## An Abundance of the Good Fat

In 1999 researchers discovered another health benefit of grass-fed products: They're the richest known source of another good fat called conjugated linoleic acid or CLA. CLA may be one of our most potent cancer fighters. Animals given very small amounts of CLA—a mere 1.5 percent of their total calories—had a 60 percent reduction in tumor growth in a study published in *Cancer Research*. CLA may fight cancer in people, as well. Recently Finnish researchers found that the more CLA in a woman's diet, the lower her risk of breast cancer. Women who consumed the most CLA had an amazing 60 percent lower risk. According to the research team, "A diet composed of CLA-rich foods, particularly cheese, may protect against breast cancer in postmenopausal women."

What the researchers failed to mention is that cheese from a grass-fed ruminant has five times more CLA than cheese from a grain-fed animal, according to Tilak Dhiman—a professor in Utah State University's Animal, Dairy and Veterinary Sciences Department. Professor Dhiman estimates that if you are an omnivore you may be able to lower your risk of cancer simply by eating daily one serving of meat, one slice of cheese and one glass of milk from a grass-fed cow. If the products are from an ordinary grain-fed cow, however, you would have to eat five servings of meat, cheese and milk to reap the same benefits.

> ***"Raising animals on pasture is better for the animals, ranchers, environment and health of the consumer."***

The nutrient-rich milk from grass-fed cows is not a "designer" food that came about through genetic manipulation or the feeding of exotic ingredients: It's the milk nature provides. Whenever cattle are allowed to eat their truly traditional diet, their dairy products contain high amounts of CLA. When you switch to butter, milk and cheese from grass-fed cows, you are restoring to your diet nutrients factory farming took away.

You are also reducing your intake of something you don't want: saturated fat and calories. Feedlot operators feed grain to ruminants because it makes the animals grow faster and fatter, resulting in highly marbled meat. All that marbling adds a lot of calories. A 6-ounce steak from a grain-fed steer has almost 100 more calories than a 6-ounce steak from a grass-fed steer, according to a report in the *Journal of Food Quality*. If you eat a typical amount of beef (66.5 pounds a year), eating grass-fed beef would save you 17,733 calories a year—without requiring an ounce more of will-power. At that rate you could lose about 6 pounds a year.

## Beyond Organic

Many people confuse pasture-raised animal products with organic products. An organic label does not guarantee that animals spent most of their time on pasture. It simply means the animals had access to pasture, weren't given antibiotics, hormonal implants or injections, and their feed—whether grass, hay or grain—was organically certified. These rules allow organic meat and dairy producers to feed their animals significant amounts of grain, a proven way to speed their growth and increase milk production. The more grain in a ruminant's diet, however, the lower the amount of omega-3s, CLA, vitamin E and betacarotene in their products.

> ***"Cheese from a grass-fed ruminant has five times more [cancer-fighting acids] than cheese from a grain-fed animal."***

A pasture-based dairy farmer I know hired an independent lab to compare the amount of CLA in his cows' milk with milk from one of the leading organic dairies. The milk from his 100 percent grass-fed cows had 19 milligrams of CLA per gram of butterfat. The milk from the organic, grain-fed cows had only 5 milligrams of CLA per gram. For optimal nutrition, it's gotta be grass-fed.

Some ranchers raise their animals on organically certified pasture, the best of both worlds. When you buy products from one of these farms, you are taking home nutritious food that also meets the strict guidelines of the certifying agency.

## Less Grain, Less Pain

In addition to robbing dairy and meat products of vital nutrients, feeding grain to ruminants is stressful to the animals. Ruminants are not designed to eat large amounts of grain. All grazing animals get small amounts of grain during the time of year when grasses go to seed, but the bulk of their diet comes from green leaves. When they are fed large amounts of grain, their guts become unnaturally acidic, which can lead to a condition called subacute acidosis. A calf afflicted with this disorder will kick at its belly, eat dirt, pant, salivate excessively, go off its feed or have attacks of diarrhea.

According to an article in *Feedlot* magazine, a publication for feedlot operators, this degree of suffering is the inevitable consequence of fattening animals on grain. "Every animal in the feedlot will experience subacute acidosis at least once during the feeding period," the article says. It then reassures feedlot operators this is "an important natural function in adapting to high-grain finishing rations . . ." In other words, making calves sick to their stomachs is agribusiness-as-usual. Subacute acidosis can be much more than a bellyache, however. If the condition goes untreated, the animal will develop an ulcerated stomach and a diseased liver. It might even die.

***"For optimal nutrition, it's gotta be grass-fed."***

I am an omnivore and eat a considerable amount of meat and dairy products. But I don't want animals to suffer needlessly before they are slaughtered. I am happy to say the beef I now eat comes from an Oregon family who raises about 40 head of cattle on 120 acres of organic pasture. When the grass is growing, the animals get all their nutrients from grasses, clover and a random assortment of green plants. In the winter when the grass is dormant, the cattle eat organic hay plus a side helping of kelp for added vitamins and minerals. They are never treated with hormones, antibiotics, acid buffers or chemical additives. I have the privilege of eating meat the way nature makes it.

## Not Just for Ruminants

Ruminants are not the only animals being raised on the new pasture-based farms. Chickens, turkeys, pigs, rabbits and ducks are also being sprung from their cages and sent out to pasture. Some farmers raise five or six different species on the same pasture, bringing to mind the old family farm, replete with the clucking of hens, mooing of cows, grunting of pigs and bleating of sheep.

Nonruminants cannot live on grass alone, however. They lack the highly specialized digestive tract that would allow them to convert a diet high in roughage and low in energy into a quality meal. They need some feed in addition to grass, typically a mixture of soy and grain. But they, too, can get a significant portion of their calories from grass, ranging from 25 percent for chickens to 50 percent for ducks. The more grass the animals eat, the more omega-3 fatty acids, beta-carotene, and vitamin E in their meat and eggs.

Like ruminants, poultry and pigs raised on pasture also get to enjoy a less stressful life. This is in stark contrast to life in a confinement operation. In the worst facilities, horrific abuses can occur.

Last year, I toured a chicken "grow-out" operation—the industry term for a facility that raises chickens from day-old chicks to maturity. The husband and wife who ran the operation were contract workers for a giant conglomerate poultry producer. The couple dutifully followed all the rules handed down by the conglomerate. Indeed, they ran such a tight operation the conglomerate had designated them the second-best grow-out operation in the state. Yet if consumers had to walk through the shed before buying their chicken, my guess is that sales would plummet.

## A Carpet of Birds

I toured the operation just days before the birds were ready for market. There were 10,000 chickens crammed into each long shed, taking up every inch of floor space. When I looked down the shed, I saw a continuous carpet of white-feathered birds. I couldn't take a step without having to nudge chickens out of the way.

The chickens were sitting on a deep bed of litter. It had been fresh when the newly hatched chicks arrived, but it had not been changed in the seven weeks it had taken them to reach market size. The day I visited, the level of ammonia had risen to almost intolerable levels. I felt as if my head had been plunged into a diaper pail. The chickens were breathing air that was less than 6 inches from the litter, so the fumes must have been far worse for them.

Although I found the whole scene repellent, the U.S. government and the poultry industry do not consider these conditions abusive. It's simply the most cost-effective way to raise chickens. In a matter of days, those very birds would be slaughtered, plucked, cut into pieces, wrapped in glimmering plastic and affixed with a label proclaiming they were "fresh from the farm" and "Northwest grown."

I no longer buy commercially raised poultry, no matter how attractive the price. I won't buy animals that have been forced to breathe toxic amounts of ammonia. Fortunately I have an alternative. The chickens and turkeys I now eat come from a nearby farm where the birds are raised outdoors on organic pasture. As in nature, the birds are allowed the dignity of breathing fresh air and foraging for greens. Equally important, they have room to chase bugs, preen and sprawl outside on a sunny day. In other words, they get to be chickens. I pay twice the grocery store price for these plump, juicy birds, and I consider it a bargain.

## Good for the Planet

Raising animals on pasture is far better for the environment. One reason is obvious. In a feedlot, lots of animals deposit their manure on a small amount of bare land. When it rains, manure leaks from the piles and pollutes the nearby land and groundwater. When the manure piles up too high, it has to be trucked from the feedlot and deposited elsewhere. Given lax government regulations and the high cost of transportation, "elsewhere" is often the closest available patch of land. Manure in small quantities is an excellent fertilizer; the lush green grass on pasture-based ranches is a testimony to this fact. But in excessive amounts, manure acts as a pollutant, leaching nitrogen and phosphorous into the soil, surface water and groundwater. It is common for land surrounding large feedlot operations to be burdened with too much manure.

Some of the environmental benefits of pasturing animals are less obvious. According to Dr. Rita Schenck from the Institute of Environmental Research and Education, raising ruminants on grass may reduce greenhouse gasses. She says land kept in pasture is carpeted with plants, many of them growing year-round. As the grass grows, it draws carbon dioxide from the air and deposits it safely in the soil, a process called "carbon sequestration." Her calculations indicate a pasture-based farm may contribute to cleaner air and a healthier planet.

## Demand Fuels Supply

So where do you find environmentally friendly, animal-friendly, highly nutritious grass-fed products if you can't grow your own? Probably not—yet—in your local grocery store. Perhaps not even in a natural food store or co-op. What you will find in these outlets are "natural" and "organic" animal products, typically from animals fed a significant amount of grain. One of the largest suppliers of "natural" meat finishes their animals in feedlots on a grain diet. The main distinction between this "natural" meat and supermarket meat is the "natural" animals are not treated with hormones and antibiotics.

***"I don't want animals to suffer needlessly before they are slaughtered."***

You may have to get your grass-fed products directly from a local farmer, farmer's market or from one of the larger suppliers willing to ship products. There are pasture-based farms in every U.S. state and Canadian province. You'll probably find a supplier within a pleasant country drive of your home. For a comprehensive list of suppliers, visit eatwild.com. You'll also find lots more information about the benefits of pasture-based ranching.

For the most devout customers, driving a hundred miles to pick up their food is no obstacle. Recently a farmer who sells eggs from pastured hens told a customer in a nearby city he was out of fresh eggs. "I only have a half dozen left," he said. The customer exclaimed, "Don't sell them! I'll be there in an hour and a half!" Meat and dairy producers spend tens of millions of dollars each year in hope of generating this kind of loyalty. All it takes is a product that resonates with the customer's soul.

As awareness of the benefits of grass-fed products spreads across the country, more and more farmers will have the courage to keep their animals on the green grasses of home. The best way to support this movement and increase the availability of the products is to try some yourself. If you find them to your liking, tell a few of your friends. Good news travels fast.

# A Case for Vegetarianism

**by Jim Motavalli**

**About the author:** *Jim Motavalli is the editor of the award-winning Connecticut-based* E Magazine, *a national environmental bi-monthly. Motavalli also writes columns and articles for numerous other magazines and newspapers, including the* New York Times. *He is the author of* Forward Drive: The Race to Build "Clean" Cars for the Future *(2000) and* Breaking Gridlock: Toward Transportation that Works *(2001). In addition, Motavalli's writing on population issues won a 1999 Global Media Award from the Population Institute. Motavalli hosts a public affairs and music radio show on listener-supported WPKN-FM in Connecticut and teaches journalism at Fairfield University.*

There has never been a better time for environmentalists to become vegetarians. Evidence of the environmental impacts of a meat-based diet is piling up at the same time its health effects are becoming better known. Meanwhile, full-scale industrialized factory farming—which allows diseases to spread quickly as animals are raised in close confinement—has given rise to recent, highly publicized epidemics of meat-borne illnesses. [In 2002], the first discovery of mad cow disease in a Tokyo suburb caused beef prices to plummet in Japan and many people to stop eating meat.

All this comes at a time when meat consumption is reaching an all-time high around the world, quadrupling in the last 50 years. There are 20 billion head of livestock taking up space on the Earth, more than triple the number of people. According to the Worldwatch Institute, global livestock population has increased 60 percent since 1961, and the number of fowl being raised for human dinner tables has nearly quadrupled in the same time period, from 4.2 billion to 15.7 billion. U.S. beef and pork consumption has tripled since 1970, during which time it has more than doubled in Asia.

One reason for the increase in meat consumption is the rise of fastfood restaurants as an American dietary staple. As Eric Schlosser noted in his best-selling book *Fast Food Nation*, "Americans now spend more money on fast food—$110 billion a year—than they do on higher education. They spend more on fast

Jim Motavalli, "The Case Against Meat: Evidence Shows That Our Meat-Based Diet Is Bad for the Environment, Aggravates Global Hunger, Brutalizes Animals and Compromises Our Health," *E/The Environmental Magazine*, vol. 13, January/February 2002, p. 26. Copyright © 2002 by Earth Action Network, Inc. Reproduced by permission.

food than on movies, books, magazines, newspapers, videos and recorded music—combined."

Strong growth in meat production and consumption continues despite mounting evidence that meat-based diets are unhealthy, and that just about every aspect of meat production—from grazing-related loss of cropland and open space, to the inefficiencies of feeding vast quantities of water and grain to cattle in a hungry world, to pollution from "factory farms"—is an environmental disaster with wide and sometimes catastrophic consequences. Oregon State University agriculture professor Peter Cheeke calls factory farming "a frontal assault on the environment, with massive groundwater and air pollution problems."

***"Americans now spend more money on fast food . . . than they do on higher education."***

## World Hunger and Resources

The 4.8 pounds of grain fed to cattle to produce one pound of beef for human beings represents a colossal waste of resources in a world still teeming with people who suffer from profound hunger and malnutrition.

According to the British group Vegfam, a 10-acre farm can support 60 people growing soybeans, 24 people growing wheat, 10 people growing corn and only two producing cattle. Britain—with 56 million people—could support a population of 250 million on an all-vegetable diet. Because 90 percent of U.S. and European meat eaters' grain consumption is indirect (first being fed to animals), westerners each consume 2,000 pounds of grain a year. Most grain in underdeveloped countries is consumed directly.

While it is true that many animals graze on land that would be unsuitable for cultivation, the demand for meat has taken millions of productive acres away from farm inventories. The cost of that is incalculable. As *Diet For a Small Planet* author Frances Moore Lappe writes, imagine sitting down to an eight-ounce steak. "Then imagine the room filled with 45 to 50 people with empty bowls in front of them. For the 'feed cost' of your steak, each of their bowls could be filled with a full cup of cooked cereal grains."

Harvard nutritionist Jean Mayer estimates that reducing meat production by just 10 percent in the U.S. would free enough grain to feed 60 million people. Authors Paul and Anne Ehrlich note that a pound of wheat can be grown with 60 pounds of water, whereas a pound of meat requires 2,500 to 6,000 pounds.

## Environmental Costs

Energy-intensive U.S. factory farms generated 1.4 billion tons of animal waste in 1996, which, the Environmental Protection Agency reports, pollutes American waterways more than all other industrial sources combined. Meat production has also been linked to severe erosion of billions of acres of once-productive farmland and to the destruction of rainforests.

McDonald's took a group of British animal rights activists to court in the 1990s because they had linked the fast food giant to an unhealthy diet and rainforest destruction. The defendants, who fought the company to a standstill, made a convincing case. In court documents, the activists asserted, "From 1970 onwards, beef from cattle reared on ex-rainforest land was supplied to McDonald's." In a policy statement, McDonald's claims that it "does not purchase beef which threatens tropical rainforests anywhere in the world," but it does not deny past purchases.

According to People for the Ethical Treatment of Animals (PETA), livestock raised for food produce 130 times the excrement of the human population, some 87,000 pounds per second. The Union of Concerned Scientists points out that 20 tons of livestock manure is produced annually for every U.S. household. The much-publicized 1989 Exxon Valdez oil spill in Alaska dumped 12 million gallons of oil into Prince William Sound, but the relatively unknown 1995 New River hog waste spill in North Carolina poured 25 million gallons of excrement and urine into the water, killing an estimated 10 to 14 million fish and closing 364,000 acres of coastal shellfishing beds. Hog waste spills have caused the rapid spread of a virulent microbe called Pfiesteria piscicida, which has killed a billion fish in North Carolina alone.

> ***"Meat production has . . . been linked to severe erosion of billions of acres of once-productive farmland."***

More than a third of all raw materials and fossil fuels consumed in the U.S. are used in animal production. Beef production alone uses more water than is consumed in growing the nation's entire fruit and vegetable crop. Producing a single hamburger patty uses enough fuel to drive 20 miles and causes the loss of five times its weight in topsoil. In his book *The Food Revolution*, author John Robbins estimates that "you'd save more water by not eating a pound of California beef than you would by not showering for an entire year." Because of deforestation to create grazing land, each vegetarian saves an acre of trees per year.

"We definitely take up more environmental space when we eat meat," says Barbara Bramble of the National Wildlife Federation. "I think it's consistent with environmental values to eat lower on the food chain."

## The Human Health Toll

There is some evidence to suggest that the human digestive system was not designed for meat consumption and processing, which could help explain why there is such high incidence of heart disease, hypertension, and colon and other cancers. Add to this the plethora of drugs and antibiotics applied as a salve to unnatural factory farming conditions and growing occurrences of meat-based diseases like E. coli and Salmonella, and there's a compelling health-based case for vegetarianism.

The factory-farmed chicken, cow or pig of today is among the most medicated creatures on Earth. "For sheer overprescription, no doctor can touch the American farmer," reported *Newsweek*. According to a Centers for Disease Control and Prevention (CDC) report, the use of antimicrobial drugs for nontherapeutic purposes—mainly to increase factory farm growth rates—has risen 50 percent since 1985.

Ninety percent of commercially available eggs come from chickens raised on factory farms, and six billion "broiler" chickens emerge from the same conditions. Ninety percent of U.S.-raised pigs are closely confined at some point during their lives. According to the book *Animal Factories* by Jim Mason and Peter Singer, pork producers lose $187 million annually to chronic diseases such as dysentery, cholera, trichinosis and other ailments fostered by factory farming. Drugs are used to reduce stress levels in animals crowded together unnaturally, although 20 percent of the chickens die of stress or disease anyway.

## Contaminated Meat

One result of these conditions is a high rate of meat contamination. Up to 60 percent of chickens sold in supermarkets are infected with Salmonella entenidis, which can pass to humans if the meat is not heated to a high enough temperature. Another pathogen, Campylobacter, can also spread from chickens to human beings with deadly results.

According to the U.S. Department of Agriculture (USDA), more than 10 million animals that were dying or diseased when slaughtered were "rendered" (processed into a protein-rich meal) in 1995 for addition to pig, poultry and pet food. Animals that collapse at the slaughterhouse door or during transportation are called "downers" and their corpses are routinely processed for human consumption. A 2001 Zogby America poll conducted for the group Farm Sanctuary found that 79 percent of Americans oppose this practice, which could be an entry point for BSE into the U.S. meat supply. Farm Sanctuary petitioned the USDA in 1998 to end processing of downer meat for human consumption, but its petition was denied.

> ***"We definitely take up more environmental space when we eat meat."***

Europe will spend billions of dollars bringing a virulent epidemic of yet another animal-borne disease—foot-and-mouth—under control. In the last two years, 60 countries have had outbreaks of foot-and-mouth, which kills animals but does not spread to people.

One of the major western exports is a taste for meat, though it brings with it increased risk of heart disease and cancer. Clearly, there is something seriously wrong with a diet and food production system resulting in such waste, endemic disease and human health threats.

The average meat eater is responsible for the deaths of some 2,400 animals during his or her lifetime. Animals raised for food endure great suffering in their housing, transport, feeding and slaughter, which is something not clearly evident in the neatly wrapped packages of meat offered for sale at grocery counters. Given the information, many Americans—especially those with an environmental background—recoil at knowing they participate in a meat production system so oppressive to the animals caught up in it.

***"Up to 60 percent of chickens sold in supermarkets are infected with Salmonella entenidis."***

The family farm of the nineteenth century, with its "free-range" animals running around the farmyard or grazing in a pasture, is largely a thing of the past. Brutality to animals has become routine in today's factory farm. A recent article in the pig industry journal *National Hog Farmer* recommends reducing the average space per animal from eight to six square feet, concluding "Crowding pigs pays." Morley Safer reported on the television program *60 Minutes* that today's factory pig is no "Babe": "[They] see no sun in their limited lives, with no hay to lie on, no mud to roll in. The sows live in tiny cages, so narrow they cannot even turn around. They live over metal grates, and their waste is pushed through slats beneath them and flushed into huge pits."

Beef cattle are luckier than factory pigs in that they have an average of 14 square feet in the overcrowded feedlots where they live out their lives. Common procedures for beef calves include branding, castration and dehorning. Veal calves, taken away from their mothers shortly after birth, live their entire lives in near darkness, chained by their necks and unable to move in any direction. They commonly suffer from anemia, diarrhea, pneumonia and lameness.

Virtually all chickens today are factory raised, with as many as six egg-laying hens living in a wire-floored "battery" cage the size of an album cover. As many as 100,000 birds can live in each "henhouse." Conditions are so psychologically taxing on the birds that they must be debeaked to prevent pecking injuries. Male chicks born on factory farms—as many as 280 million per year—are simply thrown into garbage bags to die because they're of no economic value as meat or eggs.

Some 95 percent of factory-raised animals are moved by truck, where they are typically subjected to overcrowding, severe weather, hunger and thirst. Many animals die of heat exhaustion or freezing during transport.

## The Horrors of Slaughtering

Some of the worst abuse occurs at the end of the animals' lives, as documented by Gail Eisnitz' book *Slaughterhouse*, which includes interviews with slaughterhouse workers. "On the farm where I work," reports one employee, "they drag the live ones who can't stand up anymore out of the crate. They put a metal snare around her ear or foot and drag her the full length of the building.

These animals are just screaming in pain." He adds, "The slaughtering part doesn't bother me. It's the way they're treated when they're alive." Dying animals unable to walk are tossed into the "downer pile," and many suffer agonies until, after one or two days, they are finally killed.

The threat to slaughterhouse workers' safety is largely underreported or ignored in the media. For example, *Mother Jones* magazine, in an otherwise admirable story on slaughterhouse workers, barely mentions the frequent injuries caused by pain-wracked animals lashing out inside the slaughterhouses. Despite the existence of the Humane Slaughter Act and regular USDA inspection, animals are often skinned alive or—in a major threat to worker safety—regain consciousness during slaughtering.

## The Vegetarian Solution

Vegetarianism is not a new phenomenon. The ancient Greek philosopher Pythagoras was vegetarian, and until the mid-19th century, people who abstained from meat were known as "Pythagoreans." Famous followers of Pythagoras' diet included Leonardo da Vinci, Benjamin Franklin, George Bernard Shaw and Albert Einstein. The word "vegetarian" was coined in 1847 to give a name to what was then a tiny movement in England.

> ***"The average meat eater is responsible for the deaths of some 2,400 animals during his or her lifetime."***

In the U.S., the 1971 publication of *Diet For a Small Planet* was a major catalyst for introducing people to a healthy vegetarian diet. Other stimuli included Peter Singer's 1975 book *Animal Liberation*, which gave vegetarianism a moral underpinning; Singer and Jim Mason's book *Animal Factories*, the first exposé of confinement agriculture; and John Robbins' 1987 *Diet for a New America*. In the U.S., according to a 1998 *Vegetarian Journal* survey, 82 percent of vegetarians are motivated by health concerns, 75 percent by ethics, the environment and/or animal rights, 31 percent because of taste and 26 percent because of economies.

Is the vegetarian diet healthy? The common perception persists that removing meat from the menu is dangerous because of protein loss. Lapp says there is danger of protein deficiency if vegetarian diets are heavily dependent upon 1) fruit; 2) sweet potatoes or cassava (a staple root crop for more than 500 million people in the tropics); or 3) the particular western problem, junk food.

But Reed Mangels, nutrition advisor to the Vegetarian Resource Group (VRG), says vegetarians can meet their protein needs "easily" if they "eat a varied diet and consume enough calories to maintain their weight. It is not necessary to plan combinations of foods. A mixture of proteins throughout the day will provide enough 'essential amino acids.'"

Although meat is rich in protein, *Vegetarian and Vegan FAQ* reports that other good sources are potatoes, whole wheat bread, rice, broccoli, spinach, almonds, peas, chickpeas, peanut butter, tofu (soybean curd), soymilk, lentils and kale.

Supermarket shelves overflow with soy- or seitan-based meat substitutes. The soybean contains all eight essential amino acids and exceeds even meat in the amount of usable protein it can deliver to the human body. (It should be noted, however, that some people are allergic to soy, and the "hyper-processing" of some soy-based foods reduces the useful protein content.) Animal rights advocates also claim that, contrary to the urging of the meat and dairy industries, humans need to consume only two to 10 percent of their total calories as protein.

## Vegetarian Figures

How many vegetarians are there in the U.S.? It depends on whom you ask. A PETA fact sheet asserts that 12 million Americans are vegetarians, and 19,000 make the switch every week. Pamela Rice, author of *101 Reasons Why I'm a Vegetarian*, puts the number at 4.5 million, or 2.5 percent of the population, based on recent surveys. Older counts, from 1992, put the number of people who "consider themselves" to be vegetarians at seven percent of the U.S. population, or an impressive 18 million. A 1991 Gallup Poll indicated that 20 percent of the population look for vegetarian menu items when they eat out.

Actual vegetarian numbers may be lower. VRG got virtually the same results in two separate Roper Polls it sponsored in 1994 and 1997: One percent of the public, or between two and three million, is vegetarian (eats no meat or fish, but may eat dairy and/or eggs), with a third to half of them living on a vegan diet (eschewing all animal products). Roughly five percent in both studies "never eat red meat." A 2000 poll was slightly more optimistic, putting the number of vegetarians at 2.5 percent of the population. Women are more likely to be vegetarians than men; and—surprisingly—Republicans are slightly more likely to abstain from meat than Democrats.

The American Dietetic Association says in a position statement, "Appropriately planned vegetarian diets are healthful, are nutritionally adequate and provide health benefits in the prevention and treatment of certain diseases." Vegetarians now have excellent opportunities to put together well-planned meals. The sale of organic products in natural food stores is the highest growth niche in the food industry, according to *Nutrition Business Journal*, and it grew 22 percent in 1999 to $4 billion. The natural food markets of today are not the tiny storefronts of yesteryear, but full-service supermarkets, with vigorous competition among giant national chains. Diverse veggie entrees are now available in most supermarkets and on a growing list of restaurant menus.

> ***"Some of the worst abuse occurs at the end of the animals' lives."***

It's never been easier to become a vegetarian, and there have never been more compelling reasons for environmentalists to make that choice. It's not always easy to do—most environmentalists still eat meat—but the tide is beginning to turn.

# Factory Farming Is Cruel to Animals

**by Bernard E. Rollin**

**About the author:** *Bernard E. Rollin is a university distinguished professor of philosophy and animal sciences at Colorado State University in Fort Collins, Colorado.*

A young man was working for a company that operated a large, total-confinement swine farm. One day he detected symptoms of a disease among some of the feeder pigs. As a teen, he had raised pigs himself and shown them in competition, so he knew how to treat the animals. But the company's policy was to kill any diseased animals with a blow to the head—the profit margin was considered too low to allow for treatment of individual animals. So the employee decided to come in on his own time, with his own medicine, and cured the animals. The management's response was to fire him on the spot for violating company policy. Soon the young man left agriculture for good: he was weary of the conflict between what he was told to do and how he believed he should be treating the animals.

## The Effects of Confinement

Consider a sow that is being used to breed pigs for food. The overwhelming majority of today's swine are raised in severe confinement. If the "farmer" follows the recommendations of the National Pork Producers, the sow will spend virtually all of her productive life (until she is killed) in a gestation crate 2 1/2 feet wide (and sometimes 2 feet) by 7 feet long by 3 feet high. This concrete and barred cage is often too small for the 500- to 600-pound animal, which cannot lie down or turn around. Feet that are designed for soft loam are forced to carry hundreds of pounds of weight on slotted concrete. This causes severe foot and leg problems. Unable to perform any of her natural behaviors, the sow goes mad and exhibits compulsive, neurotic "stereotypical" behaviors such as bar-biting and purposeless chewing. When she is ready to birth her piglets, she is

Bernard E. Rollin, "Farm Factories: The End of Animal Husbandry," *The Christian Century*, vol. 118, December 19, 2001, p. 26. Copyright © 2001 by Christian Century Foundation. Reproduced by permission.

moved into a farrowing crate that has a creep rail so that the piglets can crawl under it and avoid being crushed by the confined sow.

Under other conditions, pigs reveal that they are highly intelligent and behaviorally complex animals. Researchers at the University of Edinburgh created a "pig park" that approximates the habitat of wild swine. Domestic pigs, usually raised in confinement, were let loose in this facility and their behavior observed. In this environment, the sows covered almost a mile in foraging, and, in keeping with their reputation as clean animals, they built carefully constructed nests on a hillside so that urine and feces ran downhill. They took turns minding each other's piglets so that each sow could forage. All of this natural behavior is inexpressible in confinement.

> ***"The overwhelming majority of today's swine are raised in severe confinement."***

Factory farming, or confinement-based industrialized agriculture, has been an established feature in North America and Europe since its introduction at the end of World War II. Agricultural scientists were concerned about supplying Americans with sufficient food. After the Dust Bowl and the Great Depression, many people had left farming. Cities and suburbs were beginning to encroach on agricultural lands, and scientists saw that the amount of land available for food production would soon diminish significantly. Farm people who had left the farm for foreign countries and urban centers during the war were reluctant to go back. "How you gonna keep 'em down on the farm now that they've seen Paree?" a song of the '40s asked. Having experienced the specter of starvation during the Great Depression, the American consumer was afraid that there would not be enough food.

At the same time, a variety of technologies relevant to agriculture were emerging, and American society began to accept the idea of technologically based economies of scale. Animal agriculture begin to industrialize. This was a major departure from traditional agriculture and its core values. Agriculture as a way of life, and agriculture as a practice of husbandry, were replaced by agriculture as an industry with values of efficiency and productivity. Thus the problems we see in confinement agriculture are not the result of cruelty or insensitivity, but the unanticipated by-product of changes in the nature of agriculture. Confinement-based agriculture contradicts basic biblical ethical teachings about animals. Yet despite the real problems in these farm factories, few Jewish and Christian leaders, theologians or ethicists have come forward to raise moral questions about them or the practices characteristic of this industry.

## The Anticruelty Ethic

The Old Testament forbids the deliberate, willful, sadistic, deviant, purposeless, intentional and unnecessary infliction of pain and suffering on animals, or outrageous neglect of them (failing to provide food and water). Biblical edicts against cruelty helped Western societies reach a social consensus on animal treatment and develop effective laws. The Massachusetts Bay colony, for example, was the first to prohibit animal cruelty, and similar laws exist today in all Western societies.

The anticruelty ethic served two purposes: it articulated concern about animal suffering caused by deviant and purposeless human actions, and it identified sadists and psychopaths who abuse animals before sometimes "graduating" to the abuse of humans. Recent research has confirmed this correlation. Many serial killers have histories of animal abuse, as do some of the teens who have shot classmates.

Biblical sources deliver a clear mandate to avoid acts of deliberate cruelty to animals. We humans are obliged, for example, to help "raise to its feet an animal that is down even if it belongs to [our] enemy" (Exodus 23:12 and Deuteronomy 22:4) We are urged not to plow an ox and an ass together because of the hardship to the weaker animal (Deut. 22:10), and to rest the animals on the sabbath when we rest (Exod. 20:10 and Exod. 23:12). Deuteronomy 25:4 forbids the muzzling of an ox when it is being used to thresh grain, for that would cause it major suffering—the animal could not partake of its favorite food, and allowing it to graze would cost the farmer virtually nothing (also in 1 Corinthians 9:9 and 1 Timothy 5:18). We are to save "a son or an ox" that has fallen into a well even if we must violate the sabbath (Luke 14:5), and to avoid killing an ox because that would be like killing a man (Isaiah 66:3).

***"Confinement-based agriculture contradicts basic biblical ethical teachings about animals."***

Other passages encourage humans to develop a character that finds cruelty abhorrent. We are to foster compassion as a virtue, and prevent insensitivity to animal suffering. The injunction against "boiling a kid in its mother's milk" (Exod. 23:19; Exod. 34:26; Deut. 14:21) is supported by Leviticus 22:26–33, which commands us not to take a very young animal from its mother, and not to slaughter an animal along with its young. The strange story of Balaam and his ass counsels against losing one's temper and beating an animal (Numbers 22) and Psalm 145 tells us that God's mercy extends over all creatures. Surely humans are being directed to follow that model.

## From Husbandry to Science

As one of my colleagues put it, "The worst thing that ever happened to my department is the name change, from Animal Husbandry to Animal Science." The practice of husbandry is the key loss in the shift from traditional to industrialized agriculture. Farmers once put animals into the environment that the animals were biologically suited for, and then augmented their natural ability to survive and thrive by providing protection from predators, food during famine, water during drought, help in birthing, protection from weather extremes, etc. Any harm or suffering inflicted on the animal resulted in harm to the producer. An animal experiencing stress or pain, for example, is not as productive or reproductively successful as a happy animal. Thus proper care and treatment of animals becomes both an ethical and prudent requirement. The producer does well if and only if the animal does well. The result is good animal husbandry: a fair and mutually beneficial contract between humans and animals, with each better off because of the relationship. Psalm 23 describes this concept of care in a metaphor so powerful that it has become the vehicle for expressing God's ideal relationship to humans.

In husbandry agriculture, individual animal productivity is a good indicator of animal well-being; in industrial agriculture, this link between productivity and well-being is severed. When productivity as an economic metric is applied to the whole operation, the welfare of the individual animal is ignored. Husbandry agriculture "put square pegs in square holes and round pegs in round holes," extending individualized care in order to create as little friction as possible. Industrial agriculture, on the other hand, forces each animal to accept the same "technological sanders"—antibiotics (which keep down disease that would otherwise spread like wildfire in close surroundings), vaccines, bacterins, hormones, air handling systems and the rest of the armamentarium used to keep the animals from dying.

Furthermore, when crowding creates unnatural conditions and elicits unnatural behaviors such as tailbiting in pigs or similar acts of cannibalism in poultry, the solution is to cut off the tail (without anesthetics) or debeak the chicken, which can cause lifelong pain.

There are four sources of suffering in these conditions:

- violation of the animals' basic needs and nature;
- lack of attention to individual animals;
- mutilation of animals to fit unnatural environments;
- an increase in diseases and other problems caused by conditions in confinement operations.

A few years ago, while visiting with some Colorado ranchers, I observed an example of animal husbandry that contrasts sharply with the experience described at the beginning of this article. That year, the ranchers had seen many of their calves afflicted with scours, a diarrheal disease. Every rancher I met had spent more money on treating the disease than was economically justified by the calves' market value. When I asked these men why they were being "economically irrational," they were adamant in their responses: "It's part of my bargain with the animal." "It's part of caring for them." This same ethical outlook leads

***"In husbandry agriculture, individual animal productivity is a good indicator of animal well-being."***

ranchers to sit up all night with sick, marginal calves, sometimes for days in a row. If they were strictly guided by economics, these people would hardly be valuing their time at 50 cents per hour—including their sleep time.

Yet industrialized swine production thrives while western cattle ranchers, the last large group of practitioners of husbandry agriculture, are an endangered species.

## Preserving Sustainability

Confinement Agriculture violates other core biblical ethical principles. It is clear that the biblical granting of "dominion" over the earth to humans means responsible stewardship, not the looting and pillaging of nature. Given that the Bible was addressed to an agrarian people, this is only common sense, and absolutely essential to preserving what we call "sustainability."

> ***"The biblical granting of 'dominion' over the earth to humans means responsible stewardship."***

Husbandry agriculture was by its very nature sustainable, unlike industrialized animal agriculture. To follow up on our swine example: When pigs (or cattle) are raised on pasture, manure becomes a benefit, since it fertilizes pasture, and pasture is of value in providing forage for animals. In industrial animal agriculture, there is little reason to maintain pasture. Instead, farmers till for grain production, thereby encouraging increased soil erosion. At the same time, manure becomes a problem, both in terms of disposal and because it leaches into the water table. Similarly, air quality in confinement operations is often a threat to both workers and animals, and animal odors drive down real property value for miles around these operations.

Another morally questionable aspect of confinement agriculture is the destruction of small farms and local communities. Because of industrialization and economy of scale, small husbandry-based producers cannot compete with animal factories. In the broiler industry, farmers who wish to survive become serfs to large operators because they cannot compete on their own. In large confinement swine operations, where the system rather than the labor force, is primary migratory, or immigrant workers hired because they are cheap, not because they possess knowledge of or concern for the animals. And those raised in a culture of husbandry, as our earlier story revealed, find it intolerable to work in the industrialized operations.

## Fighting Corporate Power

The power of confinement agriculture to pollute the earth, degrade community and destroy small, independent farmers should convince us that this type of agriculture is incompatible with biblical ethics. Furthermore, we should fear domination of the food supply by these corporate entities.

It is not necessary to raise animals this way, as history reminds us. In 1988 Sweden banned high confinement agriculture; Britain and the EU ban sow confinement. If food is destined to cost more, so be it—Americans spend an average of only 11 percent of their income on food now, while they spent more than 50 percent on food at the turn of the century. We are wrong to ignore the hidden costs paid by animal welfare, the environment, food safety and rural communities and independent farmers, and we must now add those costs to the price of our food.

If we take biblical ethics seriously, we must condemn any type of agriculture that violates the principles of husbandry. John Travis reported the following comments made by the Vatican [in] December [2000]:

> Human dominion over the natural world must not be taken as an unqualified license to kill or inflict suffering on animals. . . . The cramped and cruel methods used in the modern food industry, for example, may cross the line of morally acceptable treatment of animals . . . Marie Hendrickz, official of the Congregation for the Doctrine of the Faith, said that in view of the growing popularity of animal rights movements, the church needs to ask itself to what extent Christ's dictum, "Do to others whatever you would have them do to you," can be applied to the animal world.

It is a radical mistake to treat animals merely as products, as objects with no intrinsic value. A demand for agriculture that practices the ancient and fair contract with domestic animals is not revolutionary but conservative. As Mahatma Gandhi said, a society must ultimately be morally judged by how it treats its weakest members. No members are more vulnerable and dependent than our society's domestic animals.

Chapter 4

# Should Animals Be Used for Human Recreation?

# Chapter Preface

From household pets to circus performers, animals have long been a source of human delight and entertainment. Unfortunately, human entertainment sometimes includes pitting animals against each other or against humans in violent competitions. These battles, also known as blood sports, include dogfighting, cockfighting, and bullfighting. Animal contests, especially dogfighting, have increased dramatically in the last fifteen years. Dogfighting is perhaps the most controversial of these "sports" because of the affection many people feel for dogs.

According to the Humane Society of the United States (HSUS), "Dogfighting is a sadistic 'contest' in which two dogs—specifically bred, conditioned, and trained to fight—are placed in a pit (generally a small arena enclosed by plywood walls) to fight each other, for the spectators' gambling and entertainment." Imported from Europe in the nineteenth century, dogfighting has grown into a multimillion dollar industry. Experts contend that dogfighting occurs throughout the United States, even though the practice is illegal in all fifty states and is considered a felony in forty-six states. The HSUS estimates that dogfighting has increased about 300 percent in the last ten years. The organization also reports that about forty thousand people are involved in dogfighting nationwide.

Dogmen—owners of fighting dogs—range from professionals, to hobbyists, to amateurs. Professional dogfighters generally travel around the country and the world, breeding and fighting dogs for profit. They organize large events, usually in rural areas, follow accepted rules and regulations, and wager thousands of dollars on their dogs. Participation at this level is by invitation only, and, not surprisingly, has proven the most elusive group for authorities to prosecute. Hobbyists may have a handful of dogs that they breed, and they may follow the rules of a refereed dogfight, but, unlike professionals, they usually confine their participation to local events. Professionals and hobbyists take the breeding of their dogs seriously and value championship bloodlines. Amateurs, or street fighters, fight all breeds of dogs and normally do not keep track of a dog's fighting record or bloodlines. Street fighting between amateurs' dogs is often spontaneous and held behind an empty building with a smaller audience, although back alley fights occur with some regularity.

Dogmen use the American pit bull terrier, commonly known as a pit bull, almost exclusively in dogfights, although bulldogs, rottweilers, and mastiffs are sometimes used. The pit bull, a cross between the Staffordshire terrier and an extinct fighting bulldog, was bred in the nineteenth century for dogfighting. Since then, breeders have worked to strengthen the bloodlines of champion fighting dogs. Ideal fighters display strength, stamina, and, most importantly, "gameness." Gameness is commonly defined as an unwillingness to give up in a fight, despite severe injury and even under the threat of death. According to an anonymous dogman, "Game is the dog that won't quit fighting, the dog that'll die in the ring, the dog that'll fight with two broken legs." Dogs who display the highest levels of gameness in fights are highly prized and are the most in demand for breeding.

Animal welfare activists contend that fighting dogs experience acute suffering. Training for fights begins in puppyhood, and experts maintain that the dogs endure rigorous physical conditioning, starvation, dehydration, and often deplorable living conditions until they die in the pit or are abandoned by their owners. Training involves elaborate workout regimens, complete with treadmills (for speed and endurance) and tires or other devices to develop strong jaws. The fights themselves are particularly brutal. With their powerful jaws, pit bulls inflict severe bruising, deep puncture wounds, and broken bones on one another. Dogs often fight until one of them dies or refuses to continue. A dog who refuses to continue a fight is seen as an embarrassment to the owner; if the reluctant dog does not die in the pit, the owner frequently kills or abandons the animal. As stated by the League in Support of Animals, "To satisfy the greed and bloodlust of their owners and other spectators at these events, the unfortunate animals are forced to endure excruciating pain and suffering in bloody fights to the death."

Authorities find many abandoned dogs with the telltale scarring and disfigurement associated with dogfighting. Most of these animals must be euthanized because their history of maltreatment and dogfighting leaves them too aggressive to be trusted not to attack people or other dogs. Experts contend that society must work to end the brutal sport. In the opinion of one dogfighting opponent, "It's high time to end the brutal, inhumane pastime that may sate the bloodlust of a few people but is in the end merely dehumanizing and abhorrent." Dogfighting is not the only animal entertainment that has come under attack. The authors in the following chapter debate circuses, zoos, and other types of recreation that exploit animals for human enjoyment.

# British Fox-Hunting Should Be Preserved

**by John Fisher**

**About the author:** *John Fisher teaches at the School of Policy at the University of Newcastle in New South Wales, Australia.*

> 'Unting is all that's worth living for—all time is lost wot is not spent in 'unting—it is like the hair we breathe—if we have it not we die—it's the sport of kings, the image of war without its guilt, and only five-and-twenty per cent of its danger!
>
> —from Mr Jorrocks' first Sportin' Lector in Robert Surtees' *Handley Cross*

Mr Jorrocks' sentiments would be considered immoral rather than immortal by most people today. Fox-hunting is on a par, in public regard in Britain, less with warfare than with soccer hooliganism. Opinion polls consistently report a large majority in favour of banning hunting; the House of Commons has voted overwhelmingly to carry out the public will. Foxhunting appears indefensible because foxes meet an unpleasant death and, despite some research to the contrary, it seems likely that they are distressed by its preliminaries. It can thus be considered unethical on at least two counts: the suffering of the pursued and the desire to kill a non-human animal (to use the jargon of the animal rights movement) for sport that animates the pursuers. It appears morally equivalent to blood sports such as bearbaiting and cockfighting that have been illegal for some two centuries.

Even so, there are some differences between such activities and fox-hunting that prompt at least a sentimental plea for fox-hunting, as it existed in the past and (at least I hope) in the present. For one thing, unlike bears and cocks, foxes are vermin. They are indiscriminate killers themselves and, under the common law, every human hand has always been against them. For another, and unlike the sports now illegal, human pleasure in the hunt does not arise from the suffering of the fox. This is merely an unfortunate side-effect. And there are other legal and ethical arguments that can be deployed in its defence.

John Fisher, "British Fox-Hunting, Past and Present," *Quadrant*, vol. 46, November 2002, p. 35.
Copyright © 2002 by Quadrant Magazine Co., Ltd. Reproduced by permission of the publisher and the author.

## Contributing to the Good of Society

The main defence presently to be deployed against the threat of public sanctions is that fox-hunting is an activity freely pursued by individuals that does not impact adversely on other humans. It is possible to take this argument a step further. Although ethics and ethical systems are notoriously variable and mutable, it remains the orthodoxy, in the West at least, that a degree of suffering for a non-human animal is acceptable if it contributes to the good of human society as a whole. Adopting this premise, it will be argued below that, in the past, fox-hunting represented a public good and that there remains scope for it to do so today.

> ***"Fox-hunting is an activity freely pursued by individuals that does not impact adversely on other humans."***

The sociologist Norbert Elias uses the evolution of fox-hunting to illustrate what he calls the "civilizing process" in European history. According to Elias, growing social complexity led to a growth in refinement of manners, to greater self-control over sexuality and violence—and an emphasis "on prolonging the pleasure of the anticipatory process". He charts the evolution of fox-hunting to the eighteenth century, when not only was the pleasure of the chase prolonged, the fox was no longer killed by humans. Hounds, whose function had been to find and put up the prey, and which were bred specifically for this purpose, became the instruments of its death.

It could be argued, accepting the thesis and taking it to a logical conclusion, that the next step would be for the field to follow a drag (an artificial scent) rather than a fox. The representatives of hunting reject this on various grounds that include the end of "glorious uncertainty" and the reduction of the hunt to a mere steeplechase. In any case, however, Elias's thesis is not entirely convincing. Fox-hunting certainly became highly stylised by the eighteenth century, bound by elaborate conventions and rules. However, this was as much due to external constraints as to internal restraint. For one thing, the increasing intensity of agriculture meant, firstly, that there was little else to hunt over large parts of the country, and secondly that hunting had to be over arable and pasture rather than through waste and woodland.

Nor is the evidence for increased refinement entirely convincing. A subdued lust for killing was hardly a feature of the other country sport, shooting game birds, favoured by the landed elite. Rather, as guns improved the emphasis became on the size of the bag of birds killed. Heavy investment was made in the nineteenth century in rearing thousands of pheasants for leisured slaughter in the battle.

## An Inclusive Sport

The contrasting trends in the two sports were dramatic in fact and, for the historian, point to a paradoxical feature of the present animus against fox-hunting.

While the one (shooting) was and is necessarily exclusive, the other (hunting) was and is equally necessarily inclusive. The enjoyment of shooting could only be achieved by keeping the rest of the community at arm's length; hence the infamous Game Laws.[1] However, the pleasures of fox-hunting were, in more than theory, open to all. It was the first sport in which women participated as equals, and they did so in increasing numbers in the nineteenth century. Social class was no bar; farmers and any tradesmen who possessed a horse, which they often did, could join. Even the rural poor could and did attend the meet and some then followed on foot—or on bicycle by the end of the century.

While the actual composition of the hunt naturally took on a hierarchical nature that reflected the realities of rural society, inclusiveness was never entirely a myth in the field and, more generally, operated at a variety of levels. Thus, only the most affluent Master of Fox Hounds, as in the case of the Duke of Rutland, could afford to hunt entirely at his own expense, and even he needed the support of other land-owners, small as well as large. The hunt might seem to cross land in indiscriminate fashion, but owners had the legal right to bar access. Further, maintaining an ample supply of foxes required at least a partial creation of their favoured habitat. Landowners who did not hunt were still expected to plant and maintain gorse coverts. And the active support of other classes was just as crucial.

*"[Hunting] was and is . . . necessarily inclusive."*

The goodwill of farmers was most important. They suffered the most in direct losses from foxes and the hunt, and financial compensation from the hunt for crop and hen losses was usually a necessity. With foxes seemingly in short supply in many areas throughout the nineteenth century (one authority claims thousands were imported from France up to the 1840s), their forbearance from reacting to such losses by taking matters into their own hands was just as critical. And, with no legal restriction on vulpicide (killing foxes by means other than hounds) possible, the hunt needed the support of the whole rural society.

All the evidence suggests that this was forthcoming, and with enthusiasm. While shooting was hated by the mass of the rural population, and the Game Laws universally flouted, they took a benign and active interest in the hunt. Information was always forthcoming on the whereabouts of a fox before the hunt, or when the hounds lost their line. The meet and the hunt provided a dash of colour in the lives of all during the otherwise drab British winter.

## Hunting in Literature

Certainly, inclusivity and participation pervade the celebratory literature of hunting, one that is larger and more distinguished than for any other sport, even

1. Written in 1670, the objective of the Game Laws was to ensure that the right to hunt was reserved exclusively for the landed elite. The laws softened throughout the centuries, and by the nineteenth century, hunting was open to all who obtained a license.

cricket. From the days of Nimrod,[2] in the early nineteenth century, no sporting magazine or local newspaper (even when Radical in persuasion) was complete without accounts of hunting. Fox-hunters took pride in the peculiarly British nature of their sport, one that bemused foreigners like [Arthur] Conan Doyle's [character] Brigadier Gerard and [Anthony] Trollope's [character] American Senator. But Trollope also sought deliberately to emphasise the class-binding role of hunting—something that emerges more naturally in two of the great hunting texts.

> ***"The fox . . . is in no danger of extinction."***

At "the centre of the stories" in [Edith] Somerville and [Martin] Ross's *Experiences of an Irish R.M.*, "stands the hunt, a point where irreconcilable worlds come together". Rulers and ruled in the West of Ireland, that "Elysium of fox-hunting", unite in support of Flurry Knox, a Master of indeterminate social standing who can relate (and is related) to both. As for the orphaned [writer] Siegfried Sassoon, hunting and hunting people provided an escape from introspection and diffidence. No one has ever written better prose about any sport than Sassoon in *Memoirs of a Fox-Hunting Man.*

And then there is [Robert Smith] Surtees. While Somerville and Ross and Sassoon are still accessible to the contemporary reader, it is possible that Surtees is not. Large parts of *Handley Cross* and his other novels are unreadable, other parts incomprehensible. However, Sassoon came to hunting through Surtees, and he remains the bible for the literary fox-hunter, the creator of a world peopled by rogues, villains and fools—and of one of the great comic characters of English literature. However, while the name of Jorrocks still has resonance today, it may be for the wrong reasons.

A Goodies skit of the 1980s pilloried Jorrocks as the classic evil squire, vicious to his servants and dedicated to the slaughter of wild animals. This may be the result of ignorance; Sassoon found the gap between his fox-hunting and intellectual friends to be unbridgeable. However, John Jorrocks was in fact a Cockney grocer (witness his dropped aspirates) whose love of 'unting' (despite his cowardice confronted with a bullfinch—a combined hedge and ditch) compensates for his (multiple) vices. And the mistake (if it was one) has a significance that goes beyond mere ignorance.

## Lingering Antagonism

Even in the nineteenth century, fox-hunting and the Game Laws never lacked critics, not out of concern over fox or bird welfare but because of antipathy to the landed elite. Such antipathy was understandable; the landed classes wielded real power (even if not, as witness the repeal of the Corn Laws [a series of

2. Charles James Apperly was a nineteenth century Englishman who wrote sports articles under the byline "Nimrod."

statutes that kept the price of corn high to deter imports of cheap grain], always to their own direct advantage). They do not today, and if Britain remains a class-ridden society it is less because of any remaining deference in society than the continued vigour of inverted snobbery.

It is an unpleasant irony that this lingering antagonism finds its focus in hunting rather than shooting. This arises because, given the contrasting requirements of the sports, hunting remains an overt public activity while shooting is still private. It also reflects the massive changes to the environment within which hunting now takes place.

Victorian fox-hunters bemoaned constraints such as railways and barbed wire. Their modern counterparts face much worse, being hemmed in by the spread of suburbia, by motorways and the remorseless growth of traffic on ordinary roads (although so is the fox). Worst of all is the spread of arable at the expense of pasture, as a result of the iniquitous Common Agricultural Policy, to the partial ruin of the great hunting countries of the Quorn and the Pytchley. And the same trends have also led to the death of the society that traditionally supported hunting. Squires and parsons are virtually extinct, as are farm labourers and most of the traditional rural trades and occupations. Of the old rural triumvirate only the farmer is left, if greatly reduced in number, to provide the backbone of the modern hunt. Conversely, the fox itself is in no danger of extinction, having adapted successfully to the exigencies of modern farming and suburban sprawl.

***"[The leadership of the hunting fraternity] need now to call on the proudest tradition of the sport."***

Nevertheless, fox-hunting continues to thrive, with some 280,000 active participants today. It does so because it appeals to many outside of that traditional society; there have always been townspeople, like Mr Jorrocks, who love to hunt. And today, the future of fox-hunting lies in their hands; there is no going back to the old rural society. The leadership of the hunting fraternity still tends to be drawn from the remnants of that society which, naturally enough, sees itself as beleaguered, the inevitable victim of an ignorance that cannot be corrected. But they need now to call on the proudest tradition of the sport and take a firm stand.

The benign tradition of inclusiveness enabled Jorrocks to achieve his greatest worldly ambition. "Of all sitivations under the sun, none is more enviable, more 'onerable than that of a master of fox-'ounds. Talk of a [member of Parliament]! vot's an [member of Parliament] compared to an [master of fox hounds]." What the modern countryside needs are more figures who feel like Jorrocks. The future lies with fugitives from the town. Like Mr Jorrocks, urban migrants have three valuable characteristics. They want to live in the countryside, they enjoy country pursuits and they have money. They also represent a potential bridge to the wider community, a means of overcoming an outmoded class antagonism that remains the greatest threat to the British hunt.

# Circus Animals Are Well Treated

**by Matthew Carolan and Raymond J. Keating**

**About the author:** *Matthew Carolan is executive editor at the* National Review, *a biweekly journal that provides commentary and analysis of politics, economics, and current events. Raymond J. Keating is chief economist for the Small Business Survival Committee, a nonprofit, nonpartisan advocacy and lobbying organization for small business owners.*

No more lions, tigers and bears? Oh my! The animal rights movement wants to ban animals from that great tradition—the circus.

This issue drew our attention recently when the 110-year-old Clyde Beatty-Cole Bros. Circus came to town. [1997's] Long Island stops were Bay Shore, Oceanside, Southampton and the Smith Haven Mall.

Clowns, "an array of aerial artists" and a human cannonball brought smiles to faces of all ages, as did the circus animals, including tigers, lions, elephants, horses and dogs.

Even though these animals are well-cared for and seem quite happy, the animal rights movement says otherwise. They say circus animals are exploited, and suffer from disorientation, boredom, and "psychotic behavior." The activists want to end all animal acts in circuses.

Prior to the Smith Haven Mall show, the circus barker announced that activists were circulating petitions to get the government to ban animals from the circus. In contrast, he urged those in attendance to sign a petition declaring support "for having healthy and happy animals travel with the American Circus."

## Compelling Incentive

Circuses, of course, possess every incentive to take care of their animals. Abuse would not only risk one's livelihood but one's life as well. Mistreatment also remains unlikely, as most trainers form ties to animals, just as the rest of us do with the family dog. As the wife of a Cole Bros. elephant trainer once told

Matthew Carolan and Raymond J. Keating, "Leave the Circus Out of PC Debate," *Newsday*, August 20, 1997. Copyright © 1997 by Matthew Carolan and Raymond J. Keating. Reproduced by permission.

*Newsday*, "They can't hurt something they love so much."

Common sense would dictate that anyone concerned about animals would work with circuses, not against them.

A new report by Daniel Oliver, author of *Animal Rights: The Inhumane Crusade*, estimates that 10 million people contribute to animal rights groups to the tune of $200 million.

Many of these donors confuse animal rights groups with animal welfare organizations. "Animal welfare . . . organizations have existed for decades and seek to improve the treatment and well-being of animals," while animal rights groups "seek to end the use and ownership of animals," Oliver observes.

Animal rights groups not only argue against animals performing in circuses, they want to abolish hunting, fishing, zoos, aquariums and marine parks, dog and horse racing, rodeos and horse-drawn carriages, even tropical fish tanks or other breeding and owning of pets. Eating meat, fish, poultry or dairy also make the animal rights lengthy list of no-no's.

Most disturbing is opposition by some activists to animals being used for medical research. Over the years, animal research has played a critical role in advancing treatments and cures for many diseases, including Alzheimer's, polio, cancer, AIDS, cholera, diabetes, leprosy and smallpox, and increasing knowledge of organ-transplant and other surgical techniques.

## Differentiating Between Humans and Animals

The bottom line philosophically is that animal rights groups see no moral difference between a human being and an animal. The movement is an odd mix of moral righteousness and moral relativism. In 1991, People for the Ethical Treatment of Animals (PETA) took out an advertisement comparing meat packers to mass-murderer Jeffrey Dahmer.

At the time, PETA's lifestyles campaign director declared: "Abuse is abuse regardless of the species. We hope it will jolt a few people into realizing that what happened to those people is no different than what happens to animals."

Animals do not have rights (which would mean they could understand and carry out moral responsibilities), but humans do have a responsibility to be humane to all living creatures. That does not mean, however, that we must abandon modern advances in favor of the nature-worshipping vegetarianism of animal rights groups. (And, hey, what about plant rights?)

In such a confused age, we'll stick with the biblical injunction to man: "Rule over the fish of the sea and the birds of the air and over every living creature that moves on the ground."

When the circus comes back to Long Island, we want current and future generations to hear the roar of a lion and see the happy mayhem of the dog show. We also want our fellow man to benefit from medical research that must involve animals. Obviously, the animal rights movement has different priorities.

# Rodeo Animals Are Not Abused

**by Diana Rowe Martinez**

**About the author:** *Diana Rowe Martinez, a freelance romance and nonfiction writer, maintains a column about rodeos and cowboys at Suite101.com, a privately owned online publishing company.*

Without livestock, there would be no rodeo and the rodeo cowboy would soon be obsolete. Healthy, athletic livestock are important to the success of the rodeo cowboy. In every event, the performance of the animal makes or breaks the cowboy and will either guarantee him a win, or a loss. So it makes sense that the better the livestock is treated, the better performance it will give. Besides, cowboys and livestock go way back to the early days, the Old West. It was true then, and is today, that the animal is fed and taken care of first.

## Rules and Regulations

Members of the PRCA [Professional Rodeo Cowboys Association] believe that animals should be treated humanely, and there are rules and regulations that have been in place since 1947 to protect its animals. These rules are continually updated and include nearly 60 rules geared specifically toward the humane treatment of rodeo livestock. An entire section on Rodeo Livestock is covered in the PRCA Rule Book. The PRCA also publishes a humane facts pamphlet outlining the care and treatment of professional rodeo livestock, from which most of this lesson's information was obtained.

How can the PRCA be certain that an animal is not mistreated when they aren't around that animal every day? By inspecting every animal BEFORE it is selected for competition, the PRCA experts are able to weed out the unhealthy animals. They only want healthy and athletic animals. If an animal becomes sick or injured between the time it is drawn and the time it is scheduled for a rodeo competition, it will not be used. A sick or injured animal not only won't feel like bucking, but it can injure itself and/or the cowboy.

Diana Rowe Martinez, "Animals in Rodeo," www.suite101.com, May 7, 2001. Copyright © 2001 by Diana Rowe Martinez. Reproduced by permission.

Other checks in place require a veterinarian to be either on site or on call for every performance and every section of a slack, in the event an injury does occur. (A slack is an event that takes place outside of the 'scheduled' rodeo to narrow down the contestants for the more publicized, audience events. Slacks occur most often in larger rodeos when hundreds of cowboys enter, like Cheyenne Frontier Days or the Calgary Stampede.)

***"[Rodeo experts] only want healthy and athletic animals."***

Rodeo committees also prepare a contingency plan to move any injured animal from the arena to a location where it can be attended undisturbed and without further exciting the animal, or the crowd.

## True Experts

The true livestock experts are the cowboys and cowgirls that take care of these animals every day. Experts, men and women that care about the animals, manage PRCA rodeos. Many PRCA competitors and committee members are also veterinarians. Many have grown up on ranches and have chosen this as an alternative career, or are volunteering to be close to the profession they love. All are well educated about proper livestock care.

If at all possible, a visit behind the scenes of a rodeo would be an unmatched educational experience, or maybe tagging along with a stock contractor. The stock contractors are usually up before anyone checking on their livestock and these guys are the last to go to bed. As we've learned, the livestock is the stock contractor's livelihood, so he has an economic interest in maintaining the health of his animals.

To further protect these animals, one of the PRCA rules authorizes officials to disqualify a contestant and assess a $250 fine on the spot for unnecessary roughness—the fine doubles with each offense. Not many cowboys are willing to risk thousands of dollars of purse money.

## Looks Can Be Deceiving

But you might ask, what about all that rough stuff they do to the animals DURING the rodeo. Well, looks can be deceiving. . . .

Spurs sure look like they should hurt. According to textbooks like [S.] Sisson's *Anatomy of the Domestic Animal* and [A.A.] Maximow and [W.] Bloom's *Textbook of Histology* the hides of horses and bulls are much thicker than human skin. A person's skin is 1 to 2 mm thick; a horsehide is about 5 mm and bull hide is 7 mm thick. Plus the spurs used in professional rodeo's three riding events—bareback riding, saddle bronc riding and bull riding—must meet PRCA guidelines by having BLUNT rowels (and remember this is the star-shaped wheel on the spurs) that are one-eighth of an inch thick so as not to cut the animals. If a rider uses non-regulation spurs, he's disqualified. The rowels must be loose to roll over the horse's hide. Bull riding spurs have dull, loosely locked rowels for tighter grip on their loose hides.

The flank strap (sometimes called bucking straps) ups the bucking action and irritates the heck out of the animal. The strap consists of a sheepskin-lined strip of leather that is placed behind the horse's rib cage in the flank area. Since the strap crosses the horse's or bull's back and stomach, it is instinctual for the animals to try and throw the strap off with their hoofs as they jump and kick. According to large animal vets, these straps cause no injury to the animal. Here go those PRCA rules again. The strap MUST have a quick-release buckle and must be lined in sheepskin. Sharp or cutting objects are NEVER placed or used in the strap's construction.

What is a cattle prod? The cattle prod was originally developed by the cattle industry as a means to move their livestock. Use of the prod is seen on ranches and occasionally at the rodeo and veterinary clinics. At the PRCA rodeos, the prod is used to herd livestock into pens and chutes. PRCA rules require that the use of the prod be kept to a minimum and that the animals be only prodded on the hip or shoulder area. The prods are powered by a flashlight battery and only used for a fraction of a second. They produce 5,000–6,000 volts of electricity, but no amperage. Voltage causes burns, so this prod causes a mild shock, no injury.

***"[One survey found that] the injury rate [among rodeo animals] was so low as to be statistically negligible."***

How often are professional rodeo animals injured? According to the PRCA, a 1993–94 survey conducted at 28 PRCA rodeos indicated that the injury rate was so low as to be statistically negligible. Of the 33,991 animals entering the arena, only 16 were injured, according to data compiled by on-site vets. That translates to an injury rate of less than five-hundredths of 1 percent, or less than one animal in 2,000. All the vets taking part in the survey reported that the animals were well taken care of and the rodeo grounds were well kept. Other surveys throughout the years simply confirm that animal injury rates in professional rodeos are extremely low. . . .

Bottom line? Livestock sometimes live and eat better than the cowboys.

# British Fox-Hunting Should Be Outlawed

**by Colin Tudge**

**About the author:** *Colin Tudge is an award-winning science writer, whose articles have appeared in the* Independent, *the* Times, Natural History, *and the* New Statesman.

On the whole, I am a monarchist; but the recent sight of Prince Charles and his elder son riding with the appalling Beaufort Hunt brought out the republican in me. Fox-hunting has often been defended by intellectuals, notably by the philosopher Roger Scruton. Yet this defence betrays a deep muddle-headedness, a lack of appreciation of simple fact and of ethical and political principles which, among people in positions of influence, is truly worrying.

## Natural Predation

To begin with, defenders—including Scruton himself—argue that hunting is "natural". Predation is one of life's most fundamental facts. Nature, as [poet Alfred Lord] Tennyson remarked, is "red in tooth and claw", and everything is destined to die ("the leaves decay and fall"). Foxes, although they are hunters, are themselves hunted in the wild, as they would be now in Britain if we still had wolves. Human beings evolved as hunters, and to hunt with horses and hounds is merely to express our true nature. Protesters are effete, cut off from the gritty realities of life.

There are huge problems, both biological and ethical, with this argument. To begin with, the hunt as practised by the Beaufort and its ilk bears very little resemblance to the realities of nature. Real predators, such as lions and wolves (and indeed foxes), hunt for a living. If they don't catch anything, they don't eat. So their hunting must be cost-effective. Any failure reduces their chances of survival. But success must not be won at too high a price; natural predators must not expend more energy in the chase than the prey itself provides. If the

Colin Tudge, "Why This Scene Is Unnatural," *New Statesman*, vol. 131, February 18, 2002, p. 25.
Copyright © 2002 by New Statesman, Ltd. Reproduced by permission.

prey is too alert or elusive or fast over the ground, after a few well-judged sorties, the professional predator gives up.

The fox hunt is in absolute contrast to all of this. The hounds are fed whether they catch anything or not. The hunters, when they get back to their manors and their halls, munch out prodigiously, and then sleep it off. For them, a keen appetite and delicious torpor are the point of the endeavour. In achieving this, however, they are content to run the poor old fox to the point of exhaustion and beyond. In a real hunt, either the prey gets away fairly early and the predator gives up, or it is soon put out of its misery. The hounds are in no way comparable with wolves in the wild. They are more like domestic cats, well fed on Whiskas, who kill small birds for a hobby.

## Unlike Anything in Nature

A few years ago, Britain's stag-hunters, to their credit, commissioned the Cambridge biologist Professor Pat Bateson to assess the physical state of deer after they had been hunted with hounds. He found tissue damage far beyond anything seen in animals that had been shot, or slaughtered in an abattoir, or killed on the road. The red blood cells had broken down, releasing their haemoglobin into the blood fluid. It seems no comparable studies have been done on hunted foxes (to the fox-hunters' discredit), but it is reasonable to assume that they too are pushed beyond anything they would experience in nature. In the absence of formal data, I would guess that foxes that do escape the hunt probably die. They would be too exhausted to hunt, and the more they delayed their return to action, the worse their plight would become.

In short, the fox hunt has nothing whatever to do with nature. It is an abstraction, a pastiche of a hunt; it is the hunters, not the protesters, who are the fantasists. We might also observe in passing that horses are herbivores and in a real hunt they would be running the other way.

Perhaps most surprising, however, is that any thinking person should invoke the "hunting is natural" argument at all. After all, in the 18th century, most philosophers were at pains to demonstrate that humanity improves on nature, and that civilization improves on [philosopher Jean-Jacques] Rousseau's idea that savages are noble went very much against the grain. More generally, as [philosopher] David Hume pointed out, "natural" does not imply "right". "Ought" cannot be derived from "is". At the turn of the 20th century, the Cambridge philosopher G E Moore suggested that all attempts to derive ethical principles from direct observation of nature fall foul of what he called "the naturalistic fallacy".

## The Grand Concept of Anthropomorphism

This is where the defenders of hunting invoke the grand concept of anthropomorphism—although in two quite opposite and contradictory ways.

First, we are sternly reminded, animals are not like us. We reason and feel:

they do not. [Philosopher René] Descartes declared that thought depends on words and, as animals don't speak, therefore they cannot think. Animals, he said, are best compared to the clockwork mannequins that were popular in his day. The behaviourists, who dominated animal psychology for most of the 20th century, seemed to agree. They wanted psychology to be a science; so, they properly insisted, it must rest on direct observation and measurement. Emotions and thoughts cannot be observed directly, but behaviour can. So theory, they said, must be based on behaviour alone.

> ***"The fox hunt has nothing whatever to do with nature."***

So far so reasonable. But then the behaviourists made a terrible mistake. Soon they were declaring that because thought and feeling were too hard to measure in animals, we should assume that they do not exist. The behaviourists apparently forgot that thought and feeling had been left out only for experimental convenience. Animals should be regarded simply as complex machines, they said, as Descartes had done. To suggest they have feelings like us was to be "anthropomorphic": and for at least two generations of biologists, anthropomorphism became the cardinal sin.

Yet, by the 1980s, closer studies convinced front-line biologists that animal behaviour cannot be explained unless we suppose that they do indeed think and feel, just as "animal lovers" had insisted all along. Animals are not necessarily made happy or unhappy by the same things that move us. But happiness and unhappiness, and the ability to work things out, are certainly within the compass of the brighter beasts such as monkeys, dogs, pigs, whales and elephants. We do not understand very much about them, but the human being—a complex creature into which we do have some insight—is a better model than the clockwork toy.

Defenders of hunting have not caught up with modern psychology. On the one hand they argue, as cavalierly as 17th-century vivi-sectionists, that foxes do not think or feel so it really doesn't matter what people do to them. On the other, in the same mawkish vein of anthropomorphism that was perfected by Walt Disney, they like to suggest that "Old Reynard" belongs to the same tally-ho rustic club as they themselves and actually enjoys dicing with death on a winter afternoon. People who really should know better—such as Ted Hughes, with his "body that is bold to come" in his poem "The Thought Fox"—fall foul of such nonsense. But it is hard to improve on common sense. Anthropomorphic or not, common sense tells us that hunting with hounds is cruel, and that cruelty is bad.

## Appealing to Civil Liberties

The hunters, including Roger Scruton, now appeal to civil liberties. To hunt, they suggest, is a freedom, and freedom is one of the jewels of modern democracy. A woman on Radio 4's *The Moral Maze* once told me that my objections to fox-hunting were like those of fundamentalist Muslims, who would flay (quite literally, perhaps) the National Gallery for its nudes. For good measure, so it is often suggested, poor scholars and ne'er-do-wells like me are motivated by envy. We just do not like to see rich people having a good time. Anyway, hunting (we are assured) is not associated with class. Why, the miners of South Wales, before they became extinct, used to hunt with hounds.

Nonsense upon nonsense. Yes, liberty is a vital principle. But it does not imply carte blanche. In all societies—including those of animals—individual liberty must be tempered by respect for others. It is a fundamental principle of ethics (a matter of dogma, to be sure; but all ethics rest on dogma in the end) that no one should involve third persons in their games without those third persons' consent. Pederasty is perceived to be evil because children are not able to give informed consent and so others are able to take advantage of them. Foxes are not children, but the same principle applies. If the fox was consulted when the hunt was mustering, he surely would make known his preference to be somewhere else. As common sense and modern biology agree that foxes are sentient and intelligent, their presumed opinion matters.

Neither do I personally object to rich people having a good time. I have generally welcomed any smidgeon of the high life that has come my way. The erstwhile miners' hunt of South Wales was, if anything, even more objectionable than the pukka [first-class] version. The miners, one feels, should have stood for different ideals. (On the other hand what, besides wealth and social class, separates the tormentors of foxes from the small boys who tie fireworks to the tails of kittens? That's a great hoot, too, some say.)

> ***"Common sense tells us that hunting with hounds is cruel."***

## Contradictory Conservationists

Then there are the arguments that have to do with conservation and the rural economy. These, too, are largely self-contradictory. We are told, on the one hand, that foxes are a serious menace, and that hunting controls them; and, on the other, that the hunters are conservationists, with a deep respect for nature and animals that townies could not possibly understand.

In reality, foxes are not much of a threat (any more than the eagles were, golden and white-tailed, or the peregrines that were largely or totally eliminated by an earlier generation of hunters). They may take ornamental ducks, which can be a shame, but their main prey among livestock are chickens, which these days are mostly kept indoors. I have lost hens to foxes in my time, but always put that down to my own carelessness. My hens ran free by day, but I locked them in at night (they went inside voluntarily as darkness fell). Clearly, however, horses and hounds do not reduce the numbers significantly. Foxes, like every other wild creature, have a wonderful capacity to overbreed, and quickly fill any space that is up for grabs. Availability of food and social distance, not hunting, limit fox numbers; and when one poor wretch is hounded to an early grave, another will quickly take his place.

Oddly, the hunters' claim to conserve as well as to control is not quite so paradoxical as it seems. Often, as in traditional deer parks from China through Persia to England, and in some reserves in modern Africa and the US, herds of wild or semi-wild creatures have been maintained for hunting, sometimes for centuries. Even so, some of us feel that human beings ought to establish a different relationship with animals; and if we must appeal to tradition, then that of St Francis would be preferable. It is a sad indictment if the conservation of England's wildlife (or of Africa's elephants and rhinos) should depend on a few people's desire to kill them. Millions would like the privilege just of seeing animals in the wild, and that perhaps is the more normal instinct. In so far as conservation is bound to bow to human wishes, and has to be paid for, it surely would be better to root it in the human predilection simply for the company of animals.

> ***"Foxes are not much of a threat."***

The economic arguments don't wash either. The same class of people who form the hunters have also, this past half-century, done little or nothing to halt the mass migration of farmworkers from the countryside. Farm labour is expensive: it gets in the way of profits, and so has been cut to the bone and then some more. Government and EU [European Union] policies have been to blame, together with a slavish adherence to productivity and cash efficiency. This has not exactly been resisted by the employers. Now they shed tears for the last remaining dog handlers. But there is plenty to do in the countryside, not least to repair the damage wrought by industrial agriculture in the name of profit. It all needs financing; but if there is money for kennels, then there should be some for the countryside as a whole. As for the hounds, who will presumably disappear when hunting does, this is another of those arguments tailored for the audience. These are working dogs. They don't live as long as pets do. After a few years, they are hit on the head anyway. As country folk tell us in many another context, it doesn't pay to be sentimental. 'Tain't natural.

## The Larger Agenda

The issue of fox-hunting, though important in itself, is only part of a larger agenda. But this larger agenda is not, as the hunters maintain, rooted in woolly sentimentality, or in "ignorance", or in a hatred of pleasure, or in class envy. It is about growing up: shaking off social and psychological roots, and myths and beliefs and politics, that belong to a quite different age.

Thus, although it is surely true, as Hume and Moore insisted, that ethical standards cannot be simplistically derived from nature, ethics none the less must take account of realities. The ethical protection that we extend to children recognises the realities of childish minds. By the same token, the ethics we apply to animals should acknowledge what biologists have now shown beyond doubt: that the brighter ones (including foxes) are sentient, that they experience the widest gamut of emotions, that they do know what is happening to them. Animals are not puppets, put on earth for our delectation. Whether or not we concede that animals have "rights", we should not claim the right to chase them to exhaustion just for the sport.

More broadly still, as Sir Donald Curry acknowledges in [a] report from the Policy Commission on the Future of Farming and Food, the British countryside is a mess: not good for producers, inhabitants (human or otherwise) or visitors. The landowners who now keep hunting going have been in charge for the past one thousand years—albeit abetted and partly displaced these past few centuries by the merchant and industrial classes. They claim to be stewards of the countryside: on this rests their disdain for the townies and parvenus who dare to criticise. But the old landowners contrived to turn the country as nearly as they could into a theme park for hunting, shooting and fishing; they employed keepers to shoot and trap any putative predator whose teeth, beaks or claws threatened the creatures the themselves wanted to chase. Eagles, peregrine, owls and otters went by the board.

***"Animals are not puppets, put on earth for our delectation."***

At least the traditional landscape was picturesque, even if most of us were not allowed in. But the new industrialists are destroying even the look of it. In short, the whole countryside needs rethinking. Real biology based on observation and hypothesis must replace myth-making of the "Old Reynard" type, jolly though it may have been, except for Old Reynard himself. Humanity needs to update and generally refine its attitude to animals in the light of what modern studies tell us about them. Britain, indeed all countries in the world, need rural (and urban) policies rooted in sound ecology: in the idea that, with luck, humanity could still be here in 10,000 years, and we should make sure not to squander what there is. Democracy matters, too; and without sacrificing the wildlife, and indeed while helping and reinforcing what is left of it, we need to open up the countryside to people at large. We pay for it, after all. All this needs serious thought, and serious policies, with tight argument and real data and ethics that extend beyond our own households. Myth and feudalism have had their day. Intellectually as well as ethically, fox-hunting belongs to the philosophy of another age and is getting in the way of a better future.

# Circus Animals Are Abused

**by Marianne R. Merritt**

**About the author:** *Marianne R. Merritt is an attorney who specializes in animal law and works on matters involving the use of animals in entertainment.*

Animals in circuses suffer horribly under deplorable conditions. They are forced to live in dirty, crowded quarters; are not provided with consistent veterinary care (many circuses don't travel with veterinarians); and are trained and kept under control through the use of such devices as bullhooks (sticks with sharpened hooks at one end), clubs, whips, chains, electric "hotshot" prods, food and water deprivation, and other forms of what is unemotionally labeled "negative reinforcement." Elephants are kept in chains up to 95 percent of the time, and exotic cats and other animals are housed in small cages where they are barely given room to stand up, move around, or stretch. Baby elephants are torn from their mothers at unnaturally young ages to be trained. One (literally) shocking training method entails hosing down elephants prior to applying a hotshot, thereby making their sensitive skin even more vulnerable to pain.

Performing animals are hauled from town to town, day in and day out, in boxcars or trucks, without any ability to exercise the full range of their natural behaviors or to otherwise be left alone for any substantial period of time without being poked, prodded, and trotted out before the masses. Once they outlive their commercial usefulness, they are frequently sold to captive hunting ranches, sent to roadside zoos, auctioned off to private animal collectors, or otherwise meet dismal fates. A lucky few animals find homes at sanctuaries such as those operated by the Fund for Animals, the Performing Animal Welfare Society (PAWS), and The Elephant Sanctuary in Hohenwald (Tennessee).

Activists all over the world have taken steps to expose and prevent the abuses that occur regularly in circuses. Many U.S. animal protection groups have extensive anti-circus campaigns, and more and more state and local governments have passed or considered banning circuses with exotic animals.

To counter these measures, Ringling Bros. and other circuses have launched well-financed public-relations counterstrikes. Feld Entertainment, Ringling's

Marianne R. Merritt, "Tatters in the Big Top," *Animals' Agenda*, vol. 20, September/October 2000, pp. 38–40. Copyright © 2000 by Animal Rights Network. Reproduced by permission.

parent company, was estimated by *Fortune* magazine in 1999 to have generated more than $500 million that year from its various business ventures. A 1995 *New York Times* article estimated Ringling's advertising budget at $25 million, a figure that has likely grown in the face of court challenges and legislative hearings aimed at restricting circus activity.

## A Record of Misteatment

Ringling Bros., with its formidable pocketbook and impetus to protect its profit margin and reputation, has formed a defense based on offense. For example, it has resorted to passing out glossy pamphlets to circus patrons, claiming that its relationship with its animals is "based on constant contact, daily routines and nurturing, which foster trust and affection. Training involves a system of repetition and reward that builds on respect and reinforces the trust between animal and trainer." However, documentation provided by government inspection reports and by individuals who have worked at Ringling Bros. reveals a far grimmer picture.

For example, Ringling touts its purported success at its Center for Elephant Conservation (CEC), where it has bred ten Asian elephants. Of those offspring, however, two babies are dead: Kenny whose death resulted in the imposition of Animal Welfare Act charges that Ringling settled in 1998 for $20,000; and Benjamin, who drowned in 1999 under suspicious circumstances and who reportedly was beaten by his handlers. Of the remaining eight, two were found during a 1999 U.S. Department of Agriculture (USDA) inspection to have "large visible lesions on [their] rear legs." According to two trainers interviewed during the routine inspection, the young elephants—Doc and Angelica—suffered rope burns while being forcibly separated from their mothers. One inspection memo noted that Bill Lindsay, Ringling's chief veterinarian, attempted to downplay the seriousness of the lesions found on the babies: "Dr. Lindsay was very upset and asked repeatedly why we could not be more collegial and call him before we came. I explained to him that all our inspections are unannounced. We also asked at that time to take pictures of Doc and Angelica. All Ringling personnel were very reluctant to let us take pictures . . ." The inspectors returned to the CEC the next day to take photographs, and it was noted that the babies "appeared cleaned up." The inspectors also noticed that there were additional scars on the babies' front legs. The memo notes that Lindsay "was upset that we had even written a note about the scars and stated that we were 'silly' for making such a big issue over a little thing." Ringling Bros. called the separation method "standard industry practice," but the USDA consulted with six elephant experts about the inspection and thereafter communicated to Feld Entertainment that "we con-

> ***"Animals are housed in small cages where they are barely given room to stand up, move around, or stretch."***

sider the handling of these two elephants as reported on our inspection report of February 9–10 to be noncompliant with the Animal Welfare Act regulations. . . . we believe there is sufficient evidence that the handling of these animals caused unnecessary trauma, behavioral stress, physical harm and discomfort to these two elephants . . ."

In addition to information from government inspections, more has been learned from three former Ringling employees who have come forward with stories about the company's animal-handling practices. A complaint filed on behalf of PAWS with the USDA in April [2000] identifies Tom Rider, a former Ringling elephant handler, as an eyewitness to abuse. The complaint charges that "Mr. Rider has identified several handlers and trainers by name who he personally witnessed repeatedly beat the elephants in the Blue Unit, including the babies. Mr. Rider also traveled with the elephants on tour, and said that they live on cramped stock cars, are chained for more than 23 hours per day and exposed to extreme temperatures, and left to stand in their own waste for hours at a time."

In January 1999, another former Ringling employee, Glenn Ewell, executed an affidavit in which horrendous treatment of elephants was documented. One incident was described as follows:

"[A]fter one of the performances in Denver, one of the adult females by the name of Nicole was severely beaten by Randy and Adam because she performed poorly. The elephants were taken back to the holding area and after the other elephants were chained in place, Randy took Nicole and tried to get her to do the routine she refused to do during the performance. When Nicole refused to do the movements as instructed Randy took a bull hook and began beating Nicole in the head, on the trunk and behind the front feet. The beating continued until the handle of the bull hook shattered. While Randy was beating Nicole in the head and trunk area, Adam began beating her on the lumbar and hindquarter area on the right hand side. One of the strikes by Adam to the lumbar area resulted in the metal hook penetrating the skin and causing an open wound from which blood began flowing. After the beating was over a person by the name of Sonny doctored the wound with some type of powder to stop the bleeding. No other veterinary care was provided to my knowledge. All of the animal crew previously identified were present and witnessed the beating."

***"Elephants . . . are chained for more than 23 hours per day."***

PAWS joined by the Fund, the American Society for the Prevention of Cruelty to Animals, the Animal Welfare Institute, and two former Ringling employees has . . . filed a civil suit against Ringling Bros. for allegedly violating both the Endangered Species Act and the Animal Welfare Act in its treatment of Asian elephants.

Since 1992, 11 Ringling Bros. elephants have died in all, and other animals in the circus haven't fared much better. In February 1999, a 15-year-old horse who performed for Ringling collapsed and died shortly after being unloaded from his train car. In January 1998, a tiger confined to his cage was shot to death by a Ringling employee, apparently as payback shortly after the tiger mauled the employee's brother, the cat's trainer. The USDA issued a "serious warning" to Ringling about the incident.

> ***"Many jurisdictions and lawmakers are working to get rid of animal-based circus 'entertainment' once and for all."***

Other circuses have similarly dismal track records. In 1999, the Clyde Beatty-Cole Brothers Circus was charged with, and later settled, a complaint filed by the USDA under the auspices of the Animal Welfare Act for the "abusive use of an ankus" [bullhook] on several of its elephants. In February 2000, Clyde Beatty again was cited by the USDA for bullhook scars on two of its elephants. Indeed, the circus had been cited in January 1999 for even failing to provide the USDA with access to records pertaining to the health of its elephants. The Sterling & Reid Circus was cited in April 1999 for poking and prodding exotic cats with poles and for striking a lion across the face, as well as for leaving camels tethered in direct sunlight for a lengthy period without any shelter. The same circus, while under investigation by the USDA, turned over three of its tigers to the Oakland Zoo in 1999. Sterling & Reid also featured in its acts a trainer named Brian Franzen, who was convicted of animal cruelty charges after eight ponies in his care were seized from Sterling & Reid after being found dehydrated, malnourished, and living in substandard conditions. In 1997 in Britain, Mary Chipperfield—once considered a grand dame of the circus industry—was convicted of beating a chimpanzee with a riding crop. This is just a sampling of the recently documented abuses occurring behind the scenes.

## Recent Legislative Initiatives

Because of animal abuse and the inherent dangers of bringing wild animals in close contact with the public, many jurisdictions and lawmakers are working to get rid of animal-based circus "entertainment" once and for all. Initiatives have come before city councils on up to the U.S. Congress.

At the national level, [one] recent congressional action [was] the introduction of the Captive Elephant Accident Prevention Act, which would criminalize the use of elephants in traveling shows or for riding purposes [The Captive Elephant Accident Prevention Act is still being debated by Congress.]. As noted by the bill's sponsor, Rep. Sam Farr (D-CA), "Since 1983, at least 28 people have been killed by captive elephants performing in circuses and elephant ride exhibits. More than 70 others have been seriously injured, including at least 50 members of the general public who were spectators at circuses and other elephant exhibits. More than a dozen children have been injured, many of them hospitalized, due to elephant ride accidents."

At the state level, the Rhode Island House of Representatives passed a bill in June [2000] that would prohibit elephants, bears, tigers, and lions from being used in circuses, carnivals, and parades that perform in the state. This is the first time such a bill has been passed by a component of a state legislature, and approved despite heavy lobbying by the circus industry. The bill was not introduced into the state Senate before it recessed, but likely will be in the future. In Maryland, a bill that would have restricted the use of elephants in performances narrowly failed to pass a committee vote, but it too will probably be re-introduced.

Elsewhere, thanks to local ordinances, [as of 2000] exotic animal acts are . . . banned or tightly restricted in Corona, California; Redmond, Washington; Stamford, Connecticut; Takoma Park, Maryland; Quincy and Revere, Massachusetts; Estes Park, Colorado; Pompano Beach, Hollywood, and Lauderdale Lakes, Florida; and Collinsville, Illinois. In one of the most hotly contested debates, and one that received national media coverage, the Seattle city council nearly passed an ordinance that would have made it illegal to use exotic animals for entertainment. The circus industry lobbied heavily against the ban, and the measure failed by only one vote. However, such anti-circus activism occurring all over the country has been taking its toll on the industry. As noted in the May/June 2000 edition of *White Tops*, a circus trade periodical," [t]here were a noticeable number of cities and towns not wanting to sponsor circuses . . . "

One sign that animal circuses—particularly Ringling Bros.—know their days are numbered is the fact that Feld Entertainment has created and heavily promotes its new circus venture, Kaleidoscape, which does not use any exotic animals. As reported in a 1997 edition of *Circus Report*, another trade publication, "Times are changing, and people are changing, and maybe we need to change also; maybe animals aren't going to be in circuses because people don't want them to be. The majority will rule someday, and maybe that time is here."

## Your Agenda

When animal acts come to your town, contact the corporate and/or local sponsors and give them detailed information about what animals in circuses endure. Remind them that the informed public will link their businesses with cruelty for supporting such acts. . . .

> ***"Maybe animals aren't going to be in circuses because people don't want them to be."***

Work with local governments to get exotic animal acts banned. Contact the Animal Protection Institute for sample model legislation. Many additional organizations, such as People for the Ethical Treatment of Animals, the Performing Animal Welfare Society, The Humane Society of the United States, and the Elephant Alliance, can provide activists with tips and materials for organizing against circuses.

# Rodeos Endanger Animals

**by Eric Mills**

**About the author:** *Eric Mills is coordinator for Action for Animals and a field representative for The Fund for Animals, nonprofit organizations dedicated to fighting for animal welfare.*

The Humane Society of the US and the American Humane Association have a joint policy condemning all rodeos due to their inherent cruelty, and the negative message that such a violent activity sends, especially to children.

The Professional Rodeo Cowboys Association (PRCA), the nation's largest, sponsors some 700 rodeos annually in the US, 100 in California. The PRCA has some good humane guidelines, but they are not as strictly enforced as needed. Only recently has the PRCA adopted a rule requiring an on-site veterinarian at all its events to care for injured animals. And why not? All rodeos require on-site ambulances and paramedics to care for injured cowboys/girls. It's only fair.

## Cowboy Camaraderie

To give rodeo its due, I know of no other sport in which the contestants so unselfishly help one another. Cowboys lend the competition their horses, their saddles, and tell each other how a particular horse or bull bucks and turns, even though it might cost them the prize money. Kudos for that.

But the treatment of the animals is another story. Much of present-day rodeo is bogus from the get-go. Real cowboys never routinely rode bulls, or rode bareback, or wrestled steers, or put bucking straps on the animals (without which most would not buck), or tried to rope, throw, and tie a calf (a baby) in eight seconds flat.

The PRCA's claims notwithstanding, animal injuries are commonplace. Their own "2000 PRCA Injury Survey" documents 38 injuries at 57 PRCA rodeos that year. Five animals were killed at the California Rodeo/Salinas in 1995. [In 2001] at a July 4 rodeo in Taylorsville, California three horses were badly gored by bulls, while another bull ripped open his belly jumping a fence, endangering the audience at the same time. This is but the tip of the rodeo iceberg.

Eric Mills, "The Problem with Rodeo," *Earth Island Journal*, vol. 17, Autumn 2002, p. 48. Copyright © 2002 by Earth Island Institute. Reproduced by permission.

## Here Comes the Press

Yet rodeo continues to grow in popularity, thanks in part to increasing TV coverage and corporate sponsorship (Dodge trucks, Marlboro cigarettes, Coors beer, Coca-Cola, etc.) Coke's "Animal Welfare Policy" states that, "The Coca-Cola Company does not endorse or condone any practice of cruelty to animals, and the Company does not sponsor or promote events where there is a risk of physical harm to animals." Hypocritically, the company allows its local bottlers to sponsor rodeos across the country, which many do. Coke needs to hear from us.

***"Much of present-day rodeo is bogus from the get-go."***

ESPN's TV coverage of rodeo is disingenuous at best. The TV camera never shows the roping calves being jerked down—the camera always pans back to horse and rider, giving the false impression that the animals never get hurt. At [2001's] National Finals Rodeo in Las Vegas (a PRCA event) a horse was killed in the arena, unknown to the TV audience thanks to the miracle of "the seven-second delay." This is dishonest reporting.

## Growing Concern

There is growing public concern about rodeos generally The State of Rhode Island banned tie-down calf roping in 1989, due to its cruelty. Pittsburgh, Pennsylvania has banned painful rodeo tack such as spurs, bucking straps and electric prods, as has Leesburg, Virginia. Only [in 2001] Pasadena, California banned all circuses and rodeos. And [in 2002], the US Olympic Committee received more than 2,000 letters decrying the inclusion of an ill-advised "Olympic Rodeo" at the Winter Games in Salt Lake City.

At press time [in 2002], two state rodeo bills are wending their way through the California State Legislature. SB 1851, by Senator Don Perata, would require an on-site veterinarian at most rodeos. (A no-brainer, right? Yet, amazingly, the California Veterinary Medical Association was opposed.) The other, SB 1306, by Senator Liz Figueroa, would ban the brutal practice of "steer tailing," a standard event at "charreadas," the Mexican-style rodeos common throughout California and the Southwest. In steer-tailing, a person on horseback grabs and then bends a steer's tail in half, in an attempt to make the animal come crashing to the ground. In many cases the animal's tail is broken or even torn off. [Both bills failed.]

Rodeo is only a detour en route to the slaughterhouse for most of these animals. They (and we) deserve better.

# Zoo Animals Are Mistreated

**by Rob Laidlaw**

**About the author:** *Rob Laidlaw is executive director of Zoocheck Canada, which he helped establish in 1998. He is a specialist in captive wildlife issues and has conducted close to one thousand zoo, circus, and wildlife display inspections throughout the United States and Canada.*

In recent years, zoos have become the target of intense public scrutiny and criticism. In response, many have tried to repackage themselves as institutions devoted to wildlife conservation, public education and animal welfare. But most zoos fail to live up to their own propaganda and vast numbers of zoo animals continue to endure lives of misery and deprivation.

## The Zoo Buzzword

Nearly every zoo, from the smallest amateur operation to the largest professional facilities, claims to be making important contributions to conservation, usually through participation in endangered species captive propagation initiatives and public education programming. The zoo world buzzword of the moment is "conservation."

Yet, with an estimated 10,000 organized zoos worldwide, representing tens of thousands of human workers and billions of dollars in operating budgets, only a tiny percentage allocate the resources necessary to participate in captive propagation initiatives, and fewer still provide any real support for the in situ protection of wildlife and their natural habitat.

So far, the record on reintroductions to the wild is dismal. Only 16 species have established self-sustaining populations in the wild as a result of captive breeding efforts, and most of those programs were initiated by government wildlife agencies—not zoos. The contribution of zoos in this regard has been minimal, and often involves supplementing existing wild populations with a small number of captive-born individuals who are ill-prepared for life in the wild.

Rob Laidlaw, "Zoos: Myth and Reality," *Satya*, July 2000. Copyright © 2000 by *Satya*. Reproduced by permission.

As the futility of captive breeding as a major conservation tool becomes evident to those in the industry, many zoos are now turning to education to justify themselves. Yet, zoo claims that they teach visitors about wildlife conservation and habitat protection, and their contention that they motivate members of the public to become directly involved in wildlife conservation work, doesn't stand up to scrutiny. The truth is that scant empirical evidence exists to prove that the primary vehicle for education in most zoos—the animal in the cage—actually teaches anyone anything. In fact, viewing animals in cages may be counterproductive educationally by conveying the wrong kinds of messages to the public. Also, the legions of conservationists that zoos should have produced, if their claims were true, have never materialized.

## Humane Treatment

But there is one issue about which there appears to be widespread agreement, at least in principle. So long as wild animals are kept in captivity, they ought to be treated humanely.

Studies have shown that animals can suffer physically, mentally and emotionally. For this reason, captive environments must be complex enough to compensate for the lack of natural freedom and choice, and they must facilitate expression of natural movement and behavior patterns. This principle has been widely espoused by the modern zoo community in various articles, books and television documentaries.

Yet despite the best of intentions or claims, most animals in zoos in North America are still consigned to lead miserable lives in undersized, impoverished enclosures, both old and new, that fail to meet their biological and behavioral needs. Many in the zoo industry will bristle at this statement and point to numerous improvements in the zoo field. They'll claim they've shifted from menagerie-style entertainment centers where animals were displayed in barred, sterile, biologically irrelevant cages, to kinder, gentler, more scientifically-based kinds of institutions.

> ***"So long as wild animals are kept in captivity, they ought to be treated humanely."***

But many of the "advances" in zoo animal housing and husbandry are superficial and provide little benefit to the animals. For example, the many new, heavily promoted, Arctic "art deco," polar bear exhibits that are springing up in zoos across the continent consistently ignore the natural biology and behavior of these animals. The artificial rockwork and hard floor surfaces typically resemble a Flintstones movie set more than the natural Arctic ice and tundra habitat of polar bears. These exhibits are made for the public and dupe them into believing things are getting better. What they really achieve is more misery and deprivation.

In addition, many new exhibits are hardly larger than the sterile, barred cages of days gone by. And one look at the prison-like, off-display holding and service areas in most zoos, where many animals spend a good portion of their lives, is proof of the hypocrisy of zoo claims that things are better for the animals than they were in the past.

## Behind the Invisible Bars

If not all is well behind the invisible bars of North America's more luxurious zoos, a more transparent problem is found in the hundreds of substandard roadside zoos that dot the continent. These amateurish operations fall far below any professional standard and do nothing but cause misery and death to thousands of animals.

My own investigations have revealed animals in visible distress lying unprotected from the full glare of the hot summer sun; primates in barren cages with no opportunity to climb; groups of black bears begging for marshmallows as they sit in stagnant moats of excrement-filled water, scarred and wounded from fighting; nocturnal animals kept without shade or privacy; animals without water; and the list goes on and on.

> ***"[Roadside zoos] do nothing but cause misery and death to thousands of animals."***

Many zoos, including those that meet industry guidelines, also annually produce a predictable surplus in animals that often end up in the hands of private collectors, animal auctions, circuses and novelty acts, substandard zoos, and even "canned hunt" operations where they're shot as trophies.

A look at compliance with the zoo industry's own standards (which in the author's view do not necessarily constitute adequate standards) demonstrates how bad the situation really is. Of the estimated 200 public display facilities in Canada, only 26—slightly more than 10 percent—have been deemed to meet the standards of the Canadian Association of Zoos and Aquariums (CAZA).

In the U.S., out of the 1,800–2,000 licensed exhibitors of wild animals (which includes biomedical research institutions, breeding facilities, small exhibitors, travelling shows, educational programs using live animals, zoos and aquariums), about 175 are accredited by the American Zoo and Aquarium Association (AZA), equivalent to less than 10 percent of all facilities.

## Public Awareness

Times are changing, and with them, public attitudes. Increasingly, members of the public find the confinement of animals in substandard conditions offensive. Zoos across the continent are feeling the pressure. They have to accept that if wild animals are to be kept in captivity, their needs must be met.

Are there good captive environments where the biological and behavioral needs of animals are being satisfied? The answer is yes. A recent Zoocheck Canada survey of black bear and gray wolf facilities in North America revealed a number of outstanding exhibits where the animals displayed an extensive range of natural movements and behaviors. But they are few and far between.

Can zoos make a useful contribution to conservation and education? Again, the answer is yes. The Durrell Wildlife Conservation Trust (Jersey Zoo) in the U.K. [United Kingdom], for example, clearly shows that zoos can become leaders in conservation education and wildlife protection. But few actually do.

I can't understand why the more responsible segments of the zoo industry have not come to their senses and acknowledged the obvious—the present state of zoos is untenable. Either zoos can voluntarily adopt humane policies and practices, push for the closure of substandard facilities, and participate in advocating for laws to help wildlife, or they can be dragged kicking and screaming into the new millennium. It's their choice.

# Hunting Is Unnecessary and Destructive

**by Peter Muller**

**About the author:** *Peter Muller is chair of the Committee to Abolish Sport Hunting (CASH), an organization that strives to educate the public about the adverse effects of sport hunting on the environment.*

Is hunting part of nature? Don't animals living in a natural environment hunt? If we lead lives consistent with our own nature and in harmony with our environment, isn't it natural to hunt to obtain food? So what's wrong with hunting?

In nature, predation is a healthy and normal relationship that some species of living organisms have with others. And there is absolutely nothing wrong with it. In fact, it would be a very aberrant ecosystem that didn't provide for some sort of predatory-prey relationship among some of its species. It is an essential part of nature.

Species that are in a predator-prey relationship have adapted by evolving together in the same ecosystem so that both species benefit from that relationship. The ecosystem, as well as the predator species and the prey species would be adversely affected if predation were to cease. Nobody would benefit from an artificially limited or disrupted predation in a healthy ecosystem.

## Characteristics of Prey Species

Over time, evolving in the same ecosystem, predator and prey species have developed structural and behavioral adaptations that allow them to be healthy predators or prey animals. Just a few examples: Prey species usually are very fecund, they tend to have large litter and short gestation periods. Rodents, rats, mice, and guinea pigs are typical prey species and are, as is well known, among the most rapidly reproducing species among mammals. For example, lemmings can have litters of about six offspring every three weeks. This is nature's way of assuring that the species will survive even though many succumb to predation. Mammals that have no natural predators reproduce much slower by having

Peter Muller, "Hunting by Humans Perverse, Too Efficient—Nature Has Solutions," www.all-creatures.org, 1998. Copyright © 1998 by Committee to Abolish Sport Hunting. Reproduced by permission of Wildlife Watch.

small litters (often one birth per pregnancy) and long gestation periods. Elephants, who have no natural predators, typically give birth to one calf after a 22-month gestation period.

The structure of the eye among prey species tends to be well-suited for peripheral vision; their eyes are on the side of the head and can be rotated to be alert to a predator approaching from any direction. Among predators the eyes are in the front of the head; the eyes can focus stereoscopically to allow the predator to assess the right distance to overtake its prey. If we look at birds for example, we see these different eye structures between the raptors such as owls, hawks, and eagles as contrasted with the passerines, examples of which are sparrows, starlings, and orioles.

***"In nature, predation is a healthy and normal relationship."***

The ability to move and survive on their own shortly after birth (precocial) is again markedly more developed among the prey species than among species that have no predators. The various species have evolved these adaptations so they can all live and thrive in their ecosystem.

A natural predator will take some of the prey species but not get close to totally eradicating its prey base. . . . It is estimated that no predator species ever takes more than about 10 percent of its prey base. The kill rate for a predator attempting to take a prey animal is also low: Sometimes it is less than 10 percent, typically it is around 20 percent.

## A Symbiotic Relationship

Predation, in nature, benefits both the predator and the prey species. The predator species, and incidentally scavenging species, benefit by having their food needs met by predation. The prey species, however, also benefits. Predation will 1) remove infected and diseased individuals, and so reduce risk of further contagion and spread of parasites and 2) remove congenitally weak animals, preventing them from breeding, and thereby improving the gene pools of the prey species.

The prey species is healthier and genetically improved by having predators. The entire ecosystem benefits from this kind of continuing interspecies interaction. This is natural predation and it promotes biodiversity; it encourages the evolution of variations of species and subspecies through adaptations of both the predator and the prey species.

## Enter Man

Hunting by humans operates perversely. The kill ratio at a couple hundred feet with a semi-automatic weapon and scope is virtually 100 percent. The animal, no matter how well-adapted to escape natural predation (healthy, alert, smart, quick, etc.) has virtually no way to escape death once it is in the cross hairs of a scope mounted on a rifle. Nature's adaptive structures and behaviors that have evolved during millions of years simply count for naught when man is the hunter.

Most deer, for example, would not perceive anything that is within the effective range of a big game rifle (up to 400 yards) as a predator or a source of danger. A wolf at that distance, even though detected, would be totally ignored. Even the much smaller range of bow-hunter (about 50–75 feet) is barely of concern to deer. Deer may start to keep an eye on a hunter at that distance, but the evasion instinct doesn't kick in until it's too late.

Hunters go after healthy big animals for meat and trophies. This leaves the diseased and congenitally weak animals to breed—thereby degrading the gene pool and spreading disease. The hunted species becomes a degenerate and runty imitation of the real species that evolved in the habitat before human hunting. Hunting by humans has never under any circumstances been akin to natural predation. Using modern technology makes matters worse, but even hunting by indigenous people, before the blessings of Western civilization were bestowed on them, was just as destructive only at a slower rate. The North American mammoth and the Patagonian giant sloth are just two examples of animals that were hunted into extinction by indigenous hunters.

## The Plight of the Deer

To see exactly how hunting is destructive to an ecosystem, let's look at a specific game animal. Probably the most widely hunted animal in North America is one of the common species of deer (white-tailed, mule deer, or black-tailed with an aggregate of about 50 subspecies).

A territory has a carrying capacity for each species that has naturally evolved in that habitat. Nature has mechanisms in place to ensure that the carrying capacity that is appropriate for that species is not exceeded.

Let's assume a naturally segmented area has sufficient browse to feed a deer population of 400 animals. What would happen if one year the herd had many more births than losses due to the winter die-off and the herd's population was brought to 500?

At the start of the next rut, several mechanisms would kick in to ensure a smaller amount of fawns the following year. If deer are hungry (not starving, but not well fed either), the sexual drive of the male deer declines and the female deer stops ovulating. Since the browse is now insufficient to feed all 500 animals, a portion of the deer population would not reproduce during that season. With the normal die-off during the winter and the smaller than normal birth during the spring, the total population would be reduced to less than 500.

> ***"Hunting by humans operates perversely."***

Within a few seasons the populations would again stabilize around the capacity of the territory. If the population dropped substantially below the carrying capacity (say to 300), similar natural mechanisms would kick in to bring the population back up to the normal carrying capacity of 400. Other mechanisms (such as immigration and emigration) are used by nature to maintain the population at the carrying capacity.

## Distorting the Gender Ratio

These mechanisms with which the species have evolved have, intrinsic within them, assumptions that have been true for millions of years. Human hunting totally destroys some of these mechanisms. Normally, left to their own devices, the sex ratio of male to female animals is about 50-50. Deer are born about evenly male and female. Most "sport" or "trophy" hunters prefer to take bucks rather than does. This distorts the gender ratio of the population. Let's say it changes from 50-50 ratio to 80-20 leaving four times as many does as bucks.

> ***"Human hunting totally destroys some of [nature's] mechanisms."***

Nature's mechanisms that adjust the population to the browse will now miscalculate and cause an overpopulation. Based on 50-50 ratio, a herd of 400 will produce a maximum 50-animal net gain assuming a 100 animal winter die-off and 150-fawn increase from the remaining 150 does.

Based on an 80-20 ratio, a 400 animal herd will produce a 140 animal increase, assuming again a 100 animal winter die-off, but this time 240 does will give birth to 240 fawns instead of 150 does giving birth to 150 fawns. With the ratio distorted at 80-20, the population will increase to 540 instead of 450.

Nature now miscalculates in assuming the increase based on a 50-50 sex ratio. Now indeed catastrophic starvation and die-offs can occur.

## Rejecting Solutions

Hunting is not the cure but the cause of overpopulation and starvation. Luke Dommer, the founder of the Committee to Abolish Sport Hunting, has proposed to several state wildlife agencies that if they are serious about using hunting as a population control tool in areas where the sex ratio is already badly distorted, they should institute a doe season. (Taking no bucks but only does until the ratio is again stabilized at 50:50). All agencies have rejected that proposal thereby giving up any pretense of ecologically motivated sound wildlife management. They quite consciously and openly state that they are in business to provide the maximum number of live targets to hunters each year.

The state agencies encourage the destruction of the naturally evolved ecosystem by encouraging human hunting that balloons the population of the game species at the expense of the other species. Their management techniques, in addition to sex-ratio distortion, include removal of natural predators (e.g.

wolves, coyotes, panthers, bears) altering the natural habitat to provide additional browse for game species and destroying the habitat of non-game species. (E.g. clear-cutting and/or burning areas and sowing them with oats for deer at the expense of rabbits, voles, various reptiles and amphibians and many other non-games species).

Things sometimes go totally haywire if a species is introduced into an ecosystem where it didn't evolve. Biologists call such an organism an "exotic" animal or plant. If the exotic animal is a prey species, it may have no defenses against a local predator and be totally wiped out in the first few weeks. On the other hand, it may not have any local predators and consequently proliferate beyond the carrying capacity of the territory, causing catastrophic die-off through starvation.

If an exotic predator is introduced, the predator species itself may die out if there is no suitable local prey. Or, it may cause the extinction of local prey species who have no defenses against the exotic predator. Or, it may cause the extinction of local predators if it is more successful and out-competes the local predator species in taking the prey.

## Disastrous Consequences

Numerous examples of the consequence of introduction of exotic organisms within environments where they have not evolved can be cited: The introduction of snakes into Guam during World War II to control the rat population nearly wiped out several indigenous bird species; introducing trout for sport fishing into Lake Titicaca in Peru in the 1930s wiped out about 25 species of local fish. Those fish species were not found anywhere else in the world. There are hundreds of examples where the introduction of an exotic species had a deleterious effect on an ecosystem.

The wildlife management agencies defy sound procedure by such practices as introducing exotic game species into areas and then distorting the habitat to favor their survival at the expense of native species that have evolved in the area. E.g., stocking an area with pheasants, an Asian bird, and cutting tall timber trees needed by native raptors for perches.

The activity of human hunting is not and never has been a sustainable, mutually beneficial, predator-prey relationship. Human hunting techniques, even the most primitive ones, are far too efficient to meet the conditions required of a natural predator-prey relationship. In modern times, with new technology, the efficiency becomes totally lopsided so as to cause instant habitat degeneration. Add to this the conscious mismanagement of habitat to further degrade and obviate all natural corrective measures.

> ***"Hunting is . . . the cause of overpopulation and starvation."***

Using techniques such as sex-ratio distortion, habitat manipulation, the removal of natural predators and the introduction of exotic game species destroys biodiversity. The goal is to maximize the number of targets for human hunting, thereby destroying the naturally evolved ecosystems and putting them at the brink of total collapse.

The number of animals of game species (native and exotic) is maximized at the expense of all others. The naturally evolved mechanisms that insure biodiversity are short-circuited.

The only way that these ecosystems will survive is to prohibit human hunting and other forms of nonsustainable consumptive uses of these animals. Permit the unfettered reintroduction and re-immigration of predators (which is occurring naturally). Stop "managing" the environment of those areas. When it comes to managing the environment, our knowledge is inadequate to do an even passable job. Even given an ethically sound motivation, which the state agencies now lack, we simply don't know enough to do a better job than nature.

Rather than playing god, we are acting more like stooges, when it comes to managing ecosystems. For the sake of life on Earth, we must not allow the hunting and gun-manufacturing lobbies to continue to dictate wildlife management policies.

# Organizations to Contact

The editors have compiled the following list of organizations concerned with the issues debated in this book. The descriptions are derived from materials provided by the organizations. All have publications or information available for interested readers. The list was compiled on the date of publication of the present volume; names, addresses, phone numbers, fax numbers, and e-mail addresses may change. Be aware that many organizations take several weeks or longer to respond to inquiries, so allow as much time as possible.

**The American Anti-Vivisection Society (AAVS)**
Noble Plaza, Suite 204801, Old York Rd., Jenkintown, PA 19046-1685
(215) 887-0816 • fax: (215) 887-2088
e-mail: aavs@aavs.org • website: www.aavs.org

AAVS advocates the abolition of vivisection, opposes all types of experiments on living animals, and sponsors research on alternatives to these methods. The society produces videos and publishes numerous brochures, including *Vivisection and Dissection and the Classroom: A Guide to Conscientious Objection.* AAVS also publishes the bimonthly *AV Magazine.*

**American Association for Laboratory Animal Science (AALAS)**
9190 Crestwyn Hills Dr., Memphis, TN 38125
(901) 754-8620 • fax: (901) 753-0046
e-mail: info@aalas.org • website: www.aalas.org

AALAS collects and exchanges information on all phases of management, care, and procurement of laboratory animals. Its publications include *Contemporary Topics in Laboratory Animal Science* and *Laboratory Animal Science.*

**The American Society for the Prevention of Cruelty to Animals (ASPCA)**
424 E. 92nd St., New York, NY 10128
(212) 876-7700 • fax: (212) 348-3031
e-mail: information@aspca.org • website: www.aspca.org

The ASPCA promotes appreciation for and humane treatment of animals, encourages enforcement of anticruelty laws, and works for the passage of legislation that strengthens existing laws to further protect animals. In addition to making available books, brochures, and videos on animal issues, the ASPCA publishes *Animal Watch*, a quarterly magazine.

**The American Vegan Society**
56 Dinshah Ln., P.O. Box 369, Malaga, NJ 08328
(856) 694-2887 • fax: (856) 694-2288
website: www.americanvegan.org

The society is dedicated to advocating a purely vegetarian diet. It publishes brochures, booklets, the quarterly *American Vegan*, and books on nonviolent living and ethical eating.

**Animal League Defense Fund (ALDF)**
127 4th St., Petaluma, CA 94952
(707) 769-7771 • fax: (707) 769-0785
e-mail: info@aldf.org • website: www.aldf.org

ALDF is an organization of attorneys and law students who promote animal rights and protect the lives and interests of animals through the use of their legal skills. It publishes the *Animals' Advocate* quarterly.

**Association of Veterinarians for Animal Rights (AVAR)**
P.O. Box 208, Davis, CA 95617
(530) 759-8106 • fax: (530) 759-8116
e-mail: info@avar.org • website: www.avar.org

The AVAR works toward the acquisition of rights for all nonhuman animals by educating the public and the veterinary profession about a variety of issues concerning nonhuman animal use. The AVAR seeks reformation of the way society treats all nonhumans and an increase in environmental awareness. AVAR publishes the monthly newsletters *Alternatives* and *Directions*, as well as various booklets, position papers, and videos.

**Farm Animal Reform Movement (FARM)**
PO Box 30654, Bethesda, MD 20824
(800) ASK-FARM
e-mail: farm@farmusa.org • website: www.farmusa.org

FARM seeks to moderate and eliminate animal suffering and other adverse impacts of commercial animal production. It promotes the annual observance of March 20th as "The Great American Meatout," a day of meatless meals, and provides a variety of brochures and fact sheets for consumers and activists.

**Food Animal Concerns Trust (FACT)**
PO Box 14599, Chicago, IL 60614
(773) 525-4952 • fax: (773) 525-5226
e-mail: info@fact.cc • website: www.info.cc

FACT promotes better care of farm animals and improved farming methods to produce safer foods and focuses on the food safety problems that arise from intensive animal production. Believing that factory-farming methods should be abolished, FACT helps farmers fund operations that raise animals humanely. Its trademarks are Nest Eggs and Rambling Rose Brand free-range veal. It publishes a quarterly newsletter, *FACT Acts*, as well as fact sheets and numerous brochures and pamphlets.

**Foundation for Biomedical Research (FBR)**
818 Connecticut Ave. NW, Suite 200, Washington, DC 20006
(202) 457-0654 • fax: (202) 457-1659
e-mail: info@research.org • website: www.fbresearch.org

FBR provides information and educational programs about what it sees as the necessary and important role of laboratory animals in biomedical research and testing. Its videos include *Caring for Laboratory Animals, The New Research Environment*, and *Caring for Life.* It also publishes a bimonthly newsletter, *Foundation for Biomedical Research.*

**The Humane Society of the United States (HSUS)**
2100 L St. NW, Washington, DC 20037
(202) 452-1100 • fax: (202) 778-6132
website: www.hsus.org

HSUS works to foster respect, understanding, and compassion for all creatures. Among its many diverse efforts, it maintains programs supporting responsible pet ownership, elimination of cruelty in hunting and trapping, exposing painful uses of animals in research and testing, and abusive treatment of animals in movies, circuses, pulling contests, and racing. It campaigns for and against legislation affecting animal protection and monitors enforcement of existing animal protection statutes. HSUS publishes the quarterlies *Animal Activist Alert*, *HSUS Close-up Reports*, and *HSUS News.*

**Institute of Laboratory Animal Research (ILAR)**
500 5th St. NW, NA 687, Washington, DC 20418
(202) 334-2590 • fax: (202) 334-1687
e-mail: ilar@nas.edu • website: dels.nas.edu/ilar

Organized under the auspices of the National Academy of Sciences, ILAR advises, upon request, the federal government and other agencies concerning the use of animals in biomedical research. It prepares guidelines and policy papers on biotechnology, the use of animals in precollege education, and other topics in laboratory animal science. Its publications include *Guide for the Care and Use of Laboratory Animals* and the quarterly *ILAR News.*

**The Jane Goodall Institute (JGI)**
P.O. Box 14890, Silver Spring, MD 20911
(301) 565-0086 • fax: (301) 565-3188
e-mail: info@janegoodall.org • website: www.janegoodall.org

JGI's goals include the support and expansion of field research on wild chimpanzees, assisting studies of chimps in captive environments, conducting comparative studies of captive and free-living chimpanzees, and enriching captive chimpanzees' lives. JGI also participates in conservation programs in Africa. It publishes a quarterly newsletter.

**John Hopkins Center for Alternatives to Animal Testing (CAAT)**
111 Market Pl., Suite 840, Baltimore, MD 21202
(410) 223-1693 • fax: (410) 223-1603
e-mail: caat@jhsph.edu • website: caat.jhsph.edu

CAAT fosters the development of scientifically acceptable alternatives to animal testing for use in the development and safety evaluation of commercial and therapeutic products. The center conducts symposia for researchers and corporations. Its publications include *Alternative Methods in Toxicology, Animals and Alternatives in Testing*, and a periodic newsletter.

**National Cattlemen's Beef Association (NCA)**
9110 E. Nichols Ave., Suite 300, Centennial, CO 80112
(303) 694-0305 • fax: (303) 694-2851
e-mail: cattle@beef.org • website: www.beef.org

The NCA functions as the central agency for national public information and legislative and industry liaison for farmers, ranchers, breeders, and feeders of beef cattle. It publishes the monthly *National Cattlemen* and the weekly *Beef Business Bulletin.*

**People for the Ethical Treatment of Animals (PETA)**
501 Front St., Norfolk, VA 23510
(757) 622-7382 • fax: (757) 622-0457
website: www.peta.org

An international animal rights organization, PETA is dedicated to establishing and protecting the rights of all animals. It focuses on four areas: factory farms, research laboratories, the fur trade, and the entertainment industry. PETA promotes public education, cruelty investigations, animal rescue, celebrity involvement, and legislative and direct action. It produces numerous videos and publishes *Animal Times, Grrr!* (a magazine for children), various fact sheets, brochures, and flyers.

**Psychologists for the Ethical Treatment of Animals (PSYETA)**
PO Box 1297, Washington Grove, MD 20880
(301) 963-4751 • fax: (301) 963-4751
e-mail: fran@psyeta.org • website: www.psyeta.org

PSYETA seeks to ensure proper treatment of animals used in psychological research and education and urges revision of curricula to include ethical issues in the treatment of animals. It works to establish procedures reducing the number of animals used in experiments and has developed a tool to measure the invasiveness or severity of animal experiments. Its publications include the *PSYETA Newsletter, Humane Innovations and Alternatives*, and the journals *Society and Animals* and the *Journal of Applied Animal Welfare.*

**Vegetarian Resource Group (VRG)**
PO Box 1463, Baltimore, MD 21203
(410) 366-8343 • fax: (410) 366-8804
e-mail: vrg@vrg.org • website: www.vrg.org

VRG membership is primarily made up of health professionals, activists, and educators working with businesses and individuals to bring about healthy nutritional changes in schools, workplaces, and communities. It educates the public about vegetarianism and veganism and examines vegetarian issues as they relate to good health, animal rights, ethics, world hunger, and ecology. VRG publishes books on vegetarianism, a computer software game, and the bimonthly newsletter *Vegetarian Journal.*

# Bibliography

**Books**


Benjamin B. Beck — *Great Apes and Humans: The Ethics of Coexistence.* Washington, DC: Smithsonian Institution Press, 2001.

Paola Cavalieri and Catherine Woollard — *The Animal Question: Why Non-Human Animals Deserve Animal Rights.* New York: Oxford University Press, 2001.

Ward M. Clark — *Misplaced Compassion: The Animal Rights Movement Exposed.* Lincoln, NE: Writers Club Press, 2001.

Carl Cohen and Tom Regan — *The Animal Rights Debate.* Lanham, MD: Rowman & Littlefield, 2001.

Debra Davis — *Animal Biotechnology: Science-Based Concerns.* Washington, DC: National Academies Press, 2002.

Jan E. Dizard — *Going Wild: Hunting, Animal Rights, and the Contested Meaning of Nature.* Amherst: University of Massachusetts Press, 1999.

Michael W. Fox — *Inhumane Society: The American Way of Exploiting Animals.* New York: St. Martin's, 2001.

Gary L. Francione and Alan Watson — *Introduction to Animal Rights: Your Child or the Dog?* Philadelphia: Temple University Press, 2000.

Linda Fulton, Michelle A. Hall, and Glenn Birrenkott — *The Laboratory Chicken.* Boca Raton, FL: CRC, 2002.

Jean Swingle Greek and C. Ray Greek — *Specious Science: How Genetics and Evolution Reveal Why Medical Research on Animals Harms Humans.* New York: Continuum, 2002.

Neville G. Gregory and Temple Grandin — *Animal Welfare and Meat Science.* Cambridge, MA: CABI, 1999.

David Hancocks — *A Different Nature: The Paradoxical World of Zoos and Their Uncertain Future.* Berkeley: University of California Press, 2002.

Chris Hayhurst — *Animal Testing: The Animal Rights Debate.* New York: Rosen, 2000.

| | |
|---|---|
| Andrew Johnson | *Factory Farming.* Oxford, UK: Blackwell, 2002. |
| Randy Malamud | *Reading Zoos: Representations of Animals and Captivity.* New York: New York University Press, 1998. |
| Donna Maurer | *Vegetarianism: Movement or Moment?* Philadelphia: Temple University Press, 2002. |
| Lyle Munro | *Compassionate Beasts: The Quest for Animal Rights.* Westport, CT: Praeger, 2000. |
| Ingrid Newkirk and Chrissie Hynde | *Free the Animals: The Story of the Animal Liberation Front.* New York: Lantern, 2000. |
| David Alan Nibert, Raf Casert, and Michael W. Fox | *Animal Rights/Human Rights.* Lanham, MD: Rowman & Littlefield, 2002. |
| Lewis Petrinovich | *Darwinian Dominion: Animal Welfare and Human Interests.* Cambridge, MA: MIT Press, 2001. |
| Rod Preece | *Awe for the Tiger, Love for the Lamb: A Chronicle of Sensibility to Animals.* New York: Routledge, 2002. |
| Tom Regan | *Defending Animal Rights.* Champaign: University of Illinois Press, 2001. |
| Deborah Rudacille | *The Scalpel and the Butterfly: The Conflict Between Animal Research and Animal Protection.* Berkeley: University of California Press, 2001. |
| Matthew Scully | *Dominion.* New York: St. Martin's, 2002. |
| Kenneth J. Shapiro and Stephen L. Zawistowski | *Food Animal Husbandry and the New Millenium.* Mahwah, NJ: Lawrence Erlbaum, 2001. |
| Peter Singer | *Animal Liberation.* New York: ECCO, 2001. |
| Gary E. Varner | *In Nature's Interests? Interests, Animal Rights, and Environmental Ethics.* New York: Oxford University Press, 2002. |
| Steven M. Wise | *Drawing the Line: Science and the Case for Animal Rights.* Cambridge, MA: Perseus, 2002. |
| Steven M. Wise | *Rattling the Cage: Toward Legal Rights for Animals.* Westport, CT: Praeger, 2000. |

**Periodicals**

| | |
|---|---|
| Scott Beckstead | "In My Opinion: Misery on the Mink Farm," *Oregonian*, December 9, 2001. |
| Arthur Caplan | "The Case for Using Pigs," *Bulletin of the World Health Organization*, January 1999. |
| John Carey | "Where Have All the Animals Gone?" *International Wildlife*, November/December 1999. |
| Julie Cohen | "Monkey Puzzles," *Geographical*, May 2000. |

Rodger D. Curren and Erin H. Hills — "From Inhumane to In Vitro: The Changing Face of Science," *Animals' Agenda*, November/December 2000.

Stuart Derbyshire — "Beastly Concerns," *Spiked*, September 18, 2002.

Kevin Dolan — "Is There a Place for Animal Experiments? The Relevance of Ethics in the Controversy About Animal Use Is Unquestionable," *British Journal of Ophthalmology*, January 2002.

Richard A. Epstein — "The Next Rights Revolution? It's Bowser's Time at Last," *National Review*, November 8, 1999.

Robert Garner — "Animal Rights and Wrongs," *Chemistry and Industry*, January 4, 1999.

Frederick K. Goodwin and Adrian R. Morrison — "Science and Self-Doubt," *Reason*, October 2000.

Henry E. Heffner — "The Symbiotic Nature of Animal Research," *Perspectives in Biology and Medicine*, Autumn 1999.

Harold Hillman — "The Limits of Ethical Vegetarianism," *Free Inquiry*, Fall 1998.

Mike Hudson — "Rights Have No Place in the Animal Kingdom," *University Wire*, June 25, 1998.

John Leo — "Another Monkey Trial," *U.S. News & World Report*, September 20, 1999.

Wendy Marston — "Deer Diary: Hunters Have Become an Endangered Species, While Deer Populations Have Run Amuck," *Sciences*, November/December 1998.

Sarah Rose A. Miller — "Animal Research," *Humanist*, September 2001.

Adrian R. Morrison — "Personal Reflections on the Animal-Rights Movement," *Perspectives in Biology and Medicine*, Winter 2001.

Adrian R. Morrison — "Perverting Medical History in the Service of 'Animal Rights'," *Perspectives in Biology and Medicine*, Autumn 2002.

Wayne Pacelle — "Cruel and Unusual Punishment on the Farm," *Los Angeles Times*, January 15, 2003.

Michael Pollan — "An Animal's Place," *New York Times Magazine*, November 10, 2002.

Dwight Schuh — "We Cannot Survive as Islands," *Bowhunter*, May/June 2002.

Roger Scruton and Andrew Tyler — "Do Animals Have Rights?" *Ecologist*, March 2001.

Karyn Siegel-Maier — "Cruelty-Free Beauty," *Better Nutrition*, April 1999.

Colin Tudge — "Chimps Don't Talk, But They Do Cry," *New Statesman*, August 2, 1999.

David Welch — "Cruel, Cowardly, and Boorish," *Spectator*, March 23, 2002.

Joy Williams — "The Inhumanity of the Animal People," *Harper's*, August 1997.

Clive D.L. Wynne — "The Soul of the Ape," *American Scientist*, March 2001.

# Index